Literature Lures

LITERATURE LURES

Using Picture Books and Novels to
Motivate Middle School Readers

Nancy J. Polette

Joan Ebbesmeyer

2002
TEACHER IDEAS PRESS
Libraries Unlimited
A Division of Greenwood Publishing Group, Inc.
Greenwood Village, Colorado

TEACHER IDEAS PRESS
Libraries Unlimited
A Division of Greenwood Publishing Group, Inc.
7730 East Belleview Avenue, Suite A200
Greenwood Village, CO 80111
1-800-237-6124
www.lu.com/tip

Library of Congress Cataloging-in-Publication Data

Polette, Nancy.
    Literature lures : using picture books and novels to motivate middle school readers /
Nancy J. Polette, Joan Ebbesmeyer.
        p. cm.
    Includes bibliographical references and index.
    ISBN 1-56308-952-1 (pbk.)
        1. Literature--Study and teaching (Middle school) 2. Picture books for children. 3.
Middle school students--Books and reading. I. Ebbesmeyer, Joan. II. Title.

LB1575+
807'.1'2--dc21

                                                                                        2001050539

CONTENTS

Part 2
LURES TO LANGUAGE

INTRODUCTION

In the search for divergent approaches to a literature program, many talented picture book authors have dispelled the myth that the picture book is intended only for young readers. Instead, it is clear that creative authors and illustrators of picture books are speaking directly to young adults. *Literature Lures: Using Picture Books and Novels to Motivate Middle School Readers* provides the teacher and librarian with the ideal resource for introducing middle school and junior high school students to challenging topics through these exceptional books.

Picture books with mature themes, absorbing illustrations, and playful text can stimulate every critical thinking skill. Imagine, for example, that cows can type. Although this may seem ridiculous, Doreen Cronin's *Click, Clack Moo Cows That Type* is a thought-provoking introduction to the power of collective bargaining. Using such a clever story to introduce *The Pushcart War,* a novel by Jean Merrill, provides students with a winning combination that presents a painless course in economics.

True appreciation of the talents involved in the production of a fine picture book can come only as the student achieves a mature viewpoint. Preteens and teens can quickly grasp weighty topics through the picture book format. For example, self-identity can be explored with Molly Bang's *Goose* and *Appearing Tonight, Mary Heather Elizabeth Livingstone* by Oliver Dunrea. Clark Taylor gives a biting indictment of the drug scene in *The House That Crack Built.* Hearts, as well as minds, are awakened by Jane Cutler's *Cello of Mr. O.* and Eve Bunting's *The Wall,* both of which deal with the consequences of war. Eve Merriam exposes problems of society in *The Inner City Mother Goose.* Mind control is the topic of *The Watertower* by Gary Crew, which provides a wonderful introduction to Lois Lowry's *The Giver.* It is impossible to read these challenging books without opening new worlds of thought.

In addition to exploring challenging issues, picture books provide students with resources for exploring language. Thinking can only be as fluent as the storehouse of words one has to use. Building that storehouse is a priority in every classroom. In Part 2 of *Literature Lures*, witty picture books provide the inspiration for word play and language development. Explore anagrams and palindromes with Jon Agee's *Elvis Lives* and *So Many Dynamos,* alliteration with *Dinorella* and *Some Smug Slug* by Pamela Duncan Edwards, puns with *Hoots and Toots and Hairy Brutes* and *Nose Drops* by Larry Shles, and parodies with *Kat Kong* by Dave Pilkey and *Snow White in New York* by Fiona French. When words are confronted in imaginative settings with all their implied subtleties, students' means of communication and ability to handle ideas are deepened.

How to Use This Book

Part 1 of *Literature Lures* introduces sophisticated and challenging picture books on a variety of issues, such as civil disobedience, homelessness, suicide, and war. After sharing the picture book, questions for discussion lead to related novels. The novels can be read aloud, assigned for individual reading, used in literature circles, or employed in any fashion that fits with the instructional procedures in place. Follow-up activities can include responses written in journals, reflections, discussion groups, art activities, debates, conversations, or research using related nonfiction books, the Internet, and other appropriate library sources.

Part 2, "Lures to Language," covers literary topics such as alliteration, parody, puns, and similes. One or more picture books are followed by a writing prompt that is sure to get the creative juices flowing. Students will be inspired to check out other examples of word play books in the library.

All the books in this resource are considered examples of high-quality literature, and they address challenging topics. Take the time to pre-read any book before using it in the classroom to ensure that it is appropriate for your audience.

Objectives of Literature Lures

The books and activities in this volume will assist teachers of middle school and junior high students in meeting the following objectives:

1. To develop a love of literature and experience joy in the reading experience.

2. To increase students' desire to read.

3. To help students connect literature with their own lives.

4. To extend students' perceptions of the lives and culture of others.

5. To become familiar with the basic components of literature: character, setting, plot, theme, mood, and point of view.

6. To provide the opportunity for students to read widely in classic and contemporary selections.

7. To interpret literature through dramatic presentations.

8. To understand idioms, analogies, and words that have multiple meaning in texts.

9. To recognize literary devices (flashback, foreshadowing, etc.).

10. To recognize an author's purpose in writing.

11. To determine a text's main ideas and how those ideas are supported by details.

12. To paraphrase and summarize text.

13. To use story strategies to learn and recall ideas.

14. To use the tools of the writer's craft (metaphor, simile, personification, etc.) in their own writing.

Beyond Literature Lures

The picture books, discussion questions, novels, and lures to language in this resource provide a foundation for the teacher or librarian who is searching for ways to immerse students in the exploration of quality literature. However, this is just the beginning of a journey that will enrich readers' lives. Encourage the students to explore other books by these authors to find other topics worthy of discussion. The Internet makes this process accessible, and entering a topic or author name into a search engine will provide opportunities for further exploration. Enjoy the journey!

Part 1

ISSUES

Civil Disobedience

Connection: Civil Protest

Picture Book

Rebel by Allan Baillie. New York: Ticknor & Fields, 1995.

In wartime Burma an officious general and his "long columns of crunching, hard-faced soldiers" march into a sleepy village with tanks and guns. Soldiers smash down doors and intimidate the people. The children in the school stare helplessly as huge tanks destroy their playground. The general issues orders to the frightened villagers: "You will give me half of everything you make. The children will learn only of my heroic battles." Then a small thong sandal sails through the air from an open school window and knocks the general's hat off. He orders all of the children to line up outside to find the child with the missing thong. As he looks at the children's feet he finds that all are barefooted and the thongs have been left piled high in the school building. The resulting wave of laughter, some even from his own troops, forces the humiliated general to leave the village. This story is based on a true incident that occurred in Rangoon.

Discussion

1. Should one always obey the law? Does the decision to obey the law depend on who is making the law?

2. Describe another incident in history when a group has put itself at risk for an individual.

3. What can be done about unjust laws?

Novel

The Pushcart War by Jean Merrill. New York: Harper & Row, 1964.

"If It's A Big Job, Why Not Make It A MAMMOTH Job?" Advertising is one way the Mammoth Moving Company, along with other trucking companies, has taken over the streets of New York City. The trucks are big and the pushcarts are small, so when the trucks and pushcarts meet on the streets, guess who gets the worst of it? Maxie Hammerman, who fixes broken pushcarts, is kept extra busy with repairs. The pushcart vendors call a meeting to make plans to stop the trucks from damaging the carts. Frank the Flower, Harry the Hot Dog, General Anna, and other vendors come up with a plan to buy a ton of peas and a ton of pins to make pea tacks to shoot into the truck tires. If many trucks were stopped, people would know who was to blame for the traffic snarls. Twenty vendors take turns making the pea tacks. When the children of New York City also begin flattening truck tires, the demand for peas grows, the supply dwindles, and the price increases. Finally, when the scheme is discovered, the mayor declares that all pushcart licenses are revoked and no pushcart can do business without a license. What will they do now? Never underestimate the power of little people working together!

Creativity

Connection: The Creative Spirit

Picture Book

📖 *The Collector of Moments* by Quint Buchholz. New York: Farrar, Straus & Giroux, 1999.

Two unique artists form a wonderful friendship. Max paints hauntingly strange pictures with a secret hidden in each of them. The other artist, a boy, plays his violin, to Max's great enjoyment. The boy uses Max's upstairs apartment as a retreat where he learns some of life's important lessons from his mentor. He also discovers why the painter calls himself the "collector of moments." The seasons pass, with the bond of friendship growing between them. However, artists must always seek new images to paint, and change is inevitable as Max looks for different places and things to depict on his canvas. The boy also must improve his musical talents and decide how he will use them.

There is pain in their good-byes, but after several months the boy receives a picture from his dear friend that shows how important he is to Max and his painting. It is a picture that, like the friendship, will be treasured forever.

Discussion

1. What do you think is the most important characteristic in becoming a great artist?

2. What contributions do great artists make to a culture or an era?

3. Why should we all strive to be creative?

4. Does being creative mean we all should try to be great painters, musicians, or sculptors? Why or why not?

Novel

📖 *Chicago Blues* by Julie Reece Deaver. New York: HarperCollins, 1995.

Lissa Hastings lives in the art world, and that is exactly where she wants to be. She feels fortunate to be studying at a well-known art school in Chicago, but she has very little money and can't imagine how she could support anyone other than herself. However, that is what she must do when her alcoholic mother can no longer care for Lissa's 11-year-old sister, Marnie. Being a single parent is a new experience for Lissa, exasperating and rewarding in turn. She worries about how her art will be affected. She must make decisions about Marnie's schooling, her personal life, and having enough money. Lissa is thankful that she is able to sell art miniatures. The girls' dad arrives unexpectedly and talks about Marnie living with him. Lissa knows how stable life has been for Marnie and has misgivings about her returning to either parent. Yet she must think about her future. Everything comes to a head when their mother gives up drinking and travels to Chicago to reclaim Marnie, and Lissa does not want to give her up. Both girls must decide what direction to take.

Novel

📖 *Destiny* by Vicki Grove. New York: G. P. Putnam's Sons, 2000.

Destiny has little in her life that inspires or uplifts. She must sell potatoes to help her poverty-stricken family make ends meet. But Destiny loves art, which lights up her drab life. It also brings her closer to her teacher, Miss Valentino, who finds a job for Destiny with Mrs. Peck. Reading, gardening, and conversing with Mrs. Peck changes Destiny's life. She discovers the joy of learning about gardening and reading about the Greeks and Romans and reading the classics. Destiny loves this world, but she must always return to the poverty and hopelessness of home. She struggles to hold hope in her heart.

Differences

Connection: Marching to a Different Drummer

Picture Book

📖 *Aliens in My Nest: Squib Meets the Teen Creature* by Larry Shles. Rolling Hills Estates, CA: Jalmar, 1988.

Filled with visual and verbal puns, this is the tale of a small owl, Squib, whose big brother, Andrew, has been his teacher and mentor. When Squib returns from summer camp he discovers that Andrew has become a teenager complete with dark glasses, heavy metal chains, and a guitar. Andrew tells him, "Beat it, punk. I don't play with children anymore." Over the summer Andrew pays no attention when mom insists he go to his room and smooth his feathers. "I am who I am," Andrew tells Squib. "Bumpy, beady, clumpy and stumpy." He refuses to eat Mom's delicious butterfly wing casseroles, preferring instead pasta with crawlers and spicy swamp sauce. When Mom is at the end of her rope and Dad is cracking up, they seek the advice of a counselor who tells them that to get Andrew safely through "owldolesence" they must practice patience, respect, communication, and understanding—and DIAL 911!

Discussion

1. What does it mean to march to a different drummer?

2. What price must be paid by nonconformists?

3. What examples can you give of someone who has no choice in being outside the norm in appearance or actions?

Novel

📖 *Lizard* by Dennis Covington. New York: Laurel Leaf Books, 1993.

Because of facial deformities, Lucius Sims looks and acts different from everyone else. In fact, he is so different that others treat him like an alien. Although there is no real evidence that he is retarded, he is sent to a home for the mentally handicapped. There he is rescued by two down-and-out actors who take him with them on a tour of the South to perform the role of Caliban in *The Tempest*. Lucius's search for freedom and self leads him to wild adventures that will keep the reader riveted through the last page.

Novel

📖 *Seventh Grade Weirdo* by Lee Wardlaw. New York: Scholastic, 1992.

Rob wants to start seventh grade with a whole new image. He wants to be known as a fairly average, normal guy. But normal might be a little too much to ask, because Rob has a problem. He comes from a family of weirdoes. His five-year-old sister Winnie is a much-publicized, genuine genius. And his mother, a Winnie the Pooh addict, runs a mail order children's book business and drives a bright pink-and-white van. On the first day of school, Rob arrives at school in his mother's embarrassing van. To his horror, everyone sees him arrive—including the Shark, the school bully, who decides then and there that Rob is the perfect victim. As Rob tries to find a way to swim with a Shark without being eaten alive, get a special girl to take him seriously, and come to understand his sister-the-genius, he makes some unexpected discoveries about truth, justice—and families.

Novel

📖 *Geeks* by Jon Katz. New York: Villard Books, 2000.

Jesse, a bright teen who doesn't fit in with his peers academically or socially, reads an article on "geeks" in *Hotwired* by Jon Katz. Jesse writes to Jon and a friendship is established. Readers watch not only the growth of their relationship but also the transformation of Jesse and his equally intelligent friend, Eric. With grit and courage, these two teens celebrate their differences by courageously leaving the small town that had rejected them to seek a brighter future.

Connection: Judging by Appearances

Picture Book

📖 *Appearing Tonight, Mary Heather Elizabeth Livingstone* by Oliver Dunrea. New York: Farrar, Straus & Giroux, 2000.

Three-year-old Mary Heather Elizabeth Livingstone charms audiences night after night with her singing and dancing. Her charm is so great that she appears professionally and audiences love her. But Mary Heather is not a happy child. She leads a lonely life with no friends and a family who seem to value her talent over her uniqueness. To compensate, she eats candy—lots of candy—and becomes so heavy that she literally outgrows stardom. While she is a young woman, Mary Heather loses her parents and has to earn her living by making one-of-a-kind dolls. She continues to eat candy. But as she ages, she remembers the theater. At age 82, she decides to audition for a singing role in a musical show. When her turn comes, she sings beautifully and dances wonderfully, stunning the director and other performers. Here is a true star! This story shows how a child, when determined to do so, can control her own destiny. The story also exposes a world that frequently rejects the talented due to appearances.

Discussion

1. Which is more important, appearance or talent? Why?

2. Can a beautiful or handsome appearance be a handicap? Why or why not?

3. What is the connection between appearance and prejudice?

Novel

📖 *Belle Prater's Boy* by Ruth White. New York: Yearling Books, 1996.

Everyone says Arbutus is beautiful. In fact, her father's nickname for her before he died was Beauty. She is so disturbed by the emphasis on her looks that she renames herself Gypsy. Woodrow, her cousin who lives next door, is rejected by some people because of his crossed eyes. However, Gypsy loves him dearly. Gypsy learns that Woodrow's mother was no beauty. She also discovers that her own father killed himself because he could not accept his disfigurement caused by a fire. Gypsy's mother says that "appearances were too important to your father." He did not understand that the outside didn't matter. The young people transform as they face painful truths.

Novel

📖 *Dinky Hocker Shoots Smack* by M. E. Kerr. New York: HarperCollins, 1972.

Fifteen-year-old Dinky Hocker is overweight, can't get a date, and spends her money on food. She wants, but does not receive, loving attention from her mother. When she finally gets a boyfriend, her parents do not approve of him and stop the relationship. In her fury at their interference, Dinky scribbles "Dinky Hocker Shoots Smack" on buildings and sidewalks in her neighborhood. Dinky's life is not the only one that changes after this. Fifteen-year-old Tucker's life also changes when he meets Dinky. Tucker shows Dinky a way to become thin. He learns how "to care."

Novel

📖 *The Planet of Junior Brown* by Virginia Hamilton. New York: Simon & Schuster, 1971.

Junior Brown lives in a special world of the imagination that he creates, perhaps to escape the real world where he must cope with his 300-pound body. He is a musical genius who finds a soul mate in a homeless boy. Junior and his new friend create their own world in the cellar beneath the school, where both find solace and a comfortable world until reality intrudes.

Connection: Understanding Differences

Picture Book

📖 *Wings* by Christopher Myers. New York: Scholastic, 2000.

Ikaras is very different. Not only is he the new boy on the block, with spiked hair and multi-colored shoes, he also has wings and can fly. The other people in the neighborhood find him strange as they watch him swoop and glide through the air. His new school experiences are a disaster. The teacher makes him leave the classroom when his wings get in her way. His classmates tease and laugh at him, and he has no friends. Just when things look darkest, Ikaras finds someone who understands his plight. She knows the loneliness of being different and comes to his rescue. Magical things begin to happen when she compliments Ikaras on his unique talents and his ability to fly. He now has someone to defend him against the world. A new and joyful friendship is formed.

Discussion

1. What does it mean when someone urges you to "spread your wings?"

2. Who was Icarus in Greek mythology?

3. Humans need food, water, and shelter for survival. Is self-esteem as important a need as these three?

Novel

📖 *Randall's Wall* by Carol Fenner. New York: Bantam Skylark Book, 1990.

Randall lives in his own little world, with his drawings and his dreams. He dreams of hunting with Uncle Luke and of the deer in the woods. He draws beautiful pictures to escape the bitter reality of his home with a pale, abused mother and brutish father. He and his sisters escape from the littered yard and filthy house whenever possible. His parents are just one step ahead of the Health Department people, who eventually find out the family doesn't even have running water. Everything changes for Randall when the beautiful and fascinating Jean, who sat in the last row of his fifth grade classroom, shows him there is another way to live. She has battles of her own to fight, but she has a loving family to support her. Jean recognizes Randall's talent, and she finds a way to make others aware of it. Randall falls in love with Jean, and all his dreams begin to come true.

Novel

📖 *Strays Like Us* by Richard Peck. New York: Dial Books, 1999.

Will and Molly, two strays, live next door to each other. Molly has been left with her great-aunt Fay, and Will is a misfit. Molly struggles to understand her mother's drug addiction and why Aunt Fay feels responsible for her. Molly begins to realize that she might be with Aunt Fay for a long time. She doesn't fit in at school, but she starts to learn a lot more about the people in town and some of their strange ways. For example, there is Claude McKinney, who wanders into peoples' houses, not knowing where he is most of the time. Molly also learns that there is someone in Will's house who never shows himself. After Molly and Will learn that Will's father died of AIDS, many other secrets come to light. Will and Molly find comfort when they learn that they are not the only strays in town.

Guns and Violence

Connection: Coping with Guns and Violence

Picture Book

📖 *Just One Flick of a Finger* by Marybeth Lorbiecki. Illustrated by David Diaz. New York: Dial Books, 1996.

Jack feels his world is out of control. He has no support from his parents, and Reebo, the school bully, makes his life a living hell with threats of violence and more. Jack is determined to be so bad that no one will mess with him. Figuring that his beer-drinking father won't care if anything happens to him, Jack takes a revolver from home and shows up at school with it. Jack's best friend, Sherms, tries to talk Jack into getting rid of the gun just as Reebo shows up to threaten Jack once again. As Jack threatens Reebo with the gun, Sherms intervenes and both he and Jack are shot, although not fatally. Diaz's street mural paintings showing graffiti-covered walls serve as a stark background for this taut tale.

Discussion

1. Does violence depicted by the media promote violence in school? Why or why not?

2. The National Rifle Association says gun ownership is a right. Do you agree? Why or why not?

3. Do you think outlawing guns would decrease shootings?

Novel

📖 *One-Eyed Cat* by Paula Fox. New York: Bradbury Press, 1984.

Ned fires the gun only once. He aims at the shadow, a gray flicker in the autumn moonlight: something, nothing. Then it is gone. The gun—a Daisy air rifle—is an eleventh birthday present from Uncle Hilary. But Ned's father, the Reverend Wallis, had forbidden his son to have it. He told him to forget about the gun—and then hid it in the attic. That night, Ned creeps up the narrow stairs as if beckoned, finds the gun, and goes outside, making just a small creaking sound. When he turns back up the hill he sees a face at the attic window, watching him. Has someone heard? His father? His spry-minded mother, who can barely rise unaided from her wheelchair? Or the dreaded Mrs. Scallop, who, in Ned's opinion, is easily the worst of all the Wallises' housekeepers? No one punishes Ned for his disobedience. But a cat turns up nearby at Mr. Scully's woodshed, a one-eyed cat that shakes its head constantly as though there is something that makes seeing difficult. Ned wonders if the cat seeks him in revenge for the injured eye. When spring comes, the shadows of Ned's uncertainties are dispelled, even as their mystery deepens, on still another moonlit night.

Novel

📖 *The Rifle* by Gary Paulsen. New York: Delacorte Press, 1991.

In 1768, a gunsmith named Cornish McManus builds a rifle of such accuracy that he knows he can never create another like it. He intends to treasure his masterpiece, but with a new wife to provide for, he feels pressed to sell it. Soon the rifle is helping John Bynam become a legendary sharpshooter in the American Revolution. When Bynam succumbs to dysentery, the weapon is passed on from owner to owner for the next two hundred years until in the twentieth century it is exchanged by a gun fanatic for an Elvis-on-velvet painting. Strangely, in all the years that the rifle was passed around and with all the people who looked at it and held it to their shoulders, not once had anyone thought to see if it was loaded. It was, and ultimately it is involved in a freak accident in which a teen is killed.

The Holocaust

Connection: Gentiles Saving Jews

Picture Book

Rose Blanche by Roberto Innocenti. San Diego: Harcourt Brace, 1985.

Rose Blanche is a little girl living in a small town in Europe during World War II. She sees the trucks roll through town filled with terrified people but doesn't understand what is happening. One day while walking through the woods she enters a clearing and finds hungry children trapped behind a barbed wire fence. She gives them the little bread she has with her and each day thereafter takes the children food. Her mother cannot understand why Rose appears to grow thinner while she is taking more and more food with her for her school lunch. Finally a day comes when armed soldiers in the town leave, taking their trucks and weapons. On a foggy day, Rose makes her daily trip to take food to the children but finds them gone. A lone soldier, perhaps mistaking Rose for the enemy in the fog, raises his rifle and shoots. Rose's mother is frantic when her child does not return home that night . . . or any night thereafter.

Discussion

1. Why do you think the author gave this story such a shocking ending?

2. What efforts can be made to see that people of different beliefs share this planet peacefully?

3. Why do you think a person would give up his or her life for strangers?

Novel

📖 *Forging Freedom* by Hudson Talbott. New York: Putnam, 2000.

Jaap Penratt, a Christian, has always felt a little Jewish because of his close friendships with many of the Jewish faith. His home town, Amsterdam, in the 1930s is one of the great Jewish centers of Europe until the German forces arrive at the outbreak of World War II and begin targeting the Jewish community. Jaap's instincts are to protect his Jewish friends and neighbors from Nazi persecution, and he sets to work making fake ID cards for them. As the war progresses and the Nazis turn his beloved Amsterdam into a death trap for Jews, Jaap realizes he must take more drastic action. The scheme he devises requires having nerves of steel to outsmart the Nazis at their own game. The hardest part for him is not risking his life but deciding which other lives he dare risk. This is a dramatic account of a man who knew he must act against dark forces.

Novel

📖 *Number the Stars* by Lois Lowry. Boston: Houghton Mifflin, 1989.

Ten-year-old Annemarie Johansen and her best friend Ellen Rosen don't run home from school in 1943. Anyone running in the streets of Copenhagen is suspicious in the eyes of the Germans, who have occupied the country since 1940. Life for the girls is filled with school, rationing, food shortages, and the ever-present Nazi soldiers marching in their town. Denmark, with its kindly King Christian and no army, had no choice but to surrender early in the war. The beloved king still rides his horse through the streets each day, bringing courage to the hearts of the Danes. The soldiers never touch him. Now, a difficult life becomes unbearable. Jewish leaders in Denmark receive word from a sympathetic German official that all Jews are to be "relocated." The Johansens are desperate to help the Rosens, and Annemarie undertakes a perilous mission to save her best friend's life.

Connection: Coping with the Holocaust

Picture Book

📖 *Terrible Things: An Allegory of the Holocaust* by Eve Bunting. Illustrated by Stephen Gammell. Philadelphia: Jewish Publication Society, 1989.

The animals in the clearing are content until the Terrible Things come, capturing all creatures with feathers. Little Rabbit wonders what was wrong with feathers, but his fellow animals silence him. "Just mind your own business, Little Rabbit. We don't want them to get mad at us." Then the Terrible Things return and take the bushy tailed creatures, the creatures that swim, and every creature that sprouts quills. Finally they come back to take any creature that is white. The only creatures left are the rabbits, and there is no one to help them. Little Rabbit hides and is not caught. "If only we had stuck together," he thinks, "it could have been different."

Discussion

1. What is an allegory? How does *Terrible Things* qualify as an allegory?

2. Has the Holocaust been repeated in recent years? When? Where?

3. Cite specific instances in which responding as a group is more effective than responding as an individual.

Novel

📖 *Anne Frank: The Diary of a Young Girl* by Anne Frank. Translated by B. M. Mooyaart. New York: Doubleday, 1967.

In 1942, on her thirteenth birthday, Anne receives a diary. Several weeks later, Anne and her family go into hiding in an Amsterdam attic. Within the pages of this diary, Anne reveals the difficulties of living in close quarters with her parents, her sister, another family, and a dentist who does not approve of Anne's high spirits. The reader also learns about worn-out clothes that cannot be replaced, meager food, and what it means to live in constant fear that you and your loved ones will be discovered. Tragically, Anne is captured and dies at Bergen-Belsen, Germany, in 1945.

Novel

📖 *Children of Bach* by Eilis Dillon. New York: Charles Scribner's Sons, 1992.

Europe is a very dangerous place to be if you are Jewish during the 1940s. Peter is only a boy, but he realizes the danger from the warnings his father continues to give him as the racial and religious hatred spread throughout the continent. Peter and his family come from a cultured, Hungarian background. They love books, painting, and music. Papa always tells Peter that these things lift people above the animals and make them feel the presence of God. All three children and their parents play musical instruments and lead a pleasant, fulfilling life until the day the children return from school to find their parents gone. Peter, the eldest, knows from his father's admonitions that his parents will not return. He is relieved when his Aunt Eva eludes the police and joins the children. They struggle to escape as new laws against the Jews are enacted. A daring escape involves trusting a variety of people as they flee in a moving van. They encounter people who jeopardize their own safety to help others. Although fear and sorrow follow them, they take comfort in the beautiful music they create, which endures beyond the war.

Novel

📖 *The Grey Striped Shirt* by Jacqueline Jules. Illustrated by Mike Cressy. Los Angeles: Alef Design Group, 1993.

Frannie finds the grey-striped uniforms when she rummages through the cedar closet in Grandma's basement. Grandma is distraught at bringing back the horrible and terrifying memories of the camp. But she know it's important to keep alive the story of what happened in the Nazi concentration camps during World War II. Frannie can barely comprehend the horror of what she learns. The tale of the hunger and

Notes on contributors

Sheila Edward had researched, and taught at
and development in several British uni
Officer for the North East on this project

Frank Coffield is Professor of Education at the
Investigator of this ESRC TLRP project,
inclusion in the learning and skills sector'

Richard Steer has been Research Officer for I
2004. Previously he worked at the Co
evaluating a DfES community programm

Maggie Gregson is a Principal Lecturer in Post
at the University of Sunderland, with
professional learning

fear of the people placed in ghettoes and robbed of their homes and their belongings is unbelievable. More horrifying is the description of the box cars that took them, packed in like cattle, to the terror of Auschwitz. Frannie is overwhelmed when she hears that 1.5 million children and 4.5 million other Jews were killed in the camps. Frannie is saddened by what had happened to her grandparents, and she knows that she must grow up to tell the story so that it will never happen again.

Connection: Surviving War

Picture Book

📖 *The Butterfly* by Patricia Polacco. New York: Philomel Books, 2000.

War makes life ugly for Monique and her family in their French village during the 1940s. The German soldiers in their tall, black boots fill Monique's world with fear and dread of what each day might bring. Finding a small girl sitting on her bed in the middle of the night is a welcome change from the tedium of wartime, but the girl flees with fear in her eyes. Monique later thinks that she had imagined the girl. The saddest day comes when the Nazi soldiers arrive in their neighborhood and attack kind old Monsieur Marks before taking him away forever. His only crime was being a Jew. Soon after, the little girl appears again in the night. This time Monique follows her down to a secret room in the basement. Monique now understands that her mother is trying to save a Jewish family. She learns that the family needs to move on to the next safe house, and Monique can help in this dangerous undertaking. Monique and her mother prove their courage and compassion in saving these helpless people. They do not know what will happen as the Jews move closer to safety, but the small girl finds a way to let them know that they survived.

Discussion

1. Why have some groups of people, such as the Jews, been persecuted throughout history?

2.   What are the pros and cons to the establishment of the Jewish state in Israel?

3.   What parallels to the attempts to eradicate Jews exist in the world today?

Novel

📖 *Good Night Maman* by Norma Fox Mazer. San Diego: Harcourt Brace, 1999.

One day Karin has her home, family, school, and friends in the beautiful city of Paris. The next day her world is destroyed when the German army marches into her city and claims it for Hitler's new empire. Everyone faces their shock and pain, but Karin's family faces an additional ordeal because they are Jewish. Karin and her brother flee from the Nazis and from some of their own compatriots who would turn them in for a reward. They hide with their mother in a closet-like room for more than a year. Even this becomes too dangerous, and the children must escape. Maman has become too ill to travel with them, and they face the journey with heavy hearts. Marc and Karin eventually find a new life in America, but it is very difficult to face all the changes and be without their beloved Maman. Finally they learn that their mother died, and they remember her sacrifices that helped save their lives.

Novel

📖 *Waiting for Anya* by Michael Morpurgo. New York: Viking, 1990.

World War II is not a war for soldiers only. It also includes millions of helpless civilians who are trying to survive. Among those millions are the Jews. The Nazis' obsessive hatred includes all Jews: the elderly, young people, children, and infants. Jo is living in France when the victorious German army marches in and establishes its own set of laws, laws of hatred and death. Jo realizes that to be caught resisting means death, but when the Germans begin rounding up all the Jews in his town, he knows he cannot stand by and do nothing. Jo is a shepherd boy with a lion's courage. He finds out that there is a widow in town who is hiding Jews. He helps with a plan to move the Jews to Spain where they can find safety, but they must move quickly. The Germans are not easily fooled. They suspect everything and everyone. When a group of soldiers move into Jo's town, the situation becomes critical. To move the Jews now means risking death, but Jo knows what he must do.

Homelessness

Connection: Coping with Homelessness

Picture Book

Fly Away Home by Eve Bunting. Illustrated by Ronald Himler. New York: Clarion Books, 1991.

Circumstances are not good for Andrew and his dad. They are alone in the world with very little money. Dad can find nothing but a weekend job and they can't afford housing. Andrew and Dad make a home at the airport. They sleep in the chairs and clean up in the restrooms. Life is dismal. However, Andrew will put up with anything to be with his father, which includes staying invisible to avoid being noticed by security. Life at the airport has few bright spots, but one day Andrew finds a little bird caught inside the main terminal. He follows the bird for days, hoping it will find a way out. At last the chance comes and the bird flies through an opening to freedom. Andrew now knows that he will someday find his open door.

Discussion

1. We all know what a house is. How would you define the word *home*?

2. Do you think homeless people in large cities should be allowed to use public facilities such as parks, bus stations, and airports for their basic needs?

3. Who should be responsible for helping the homeless?

Novel

📖 *Tonight by Sea* by Francis Temple. New York: Orchard Books, 1995.

Pauli's life in Haiti is full of poverty, danger, and fear. There is no food, no work, and little hope. Most of the people think only of escape. However, Haiti means home to Pauli. She doesn't want to leave, although her parents left Haiti and Pauli behind with relatives to find freedom. Pauli's beloved uncle builds a boat. This frightens Pauli because she knows the rest of the family hopes to escape both the poverty and the thugs called Macoutes who torture and kill anyone who opposes them. When Pauli's best friend is killed by the terrorists, she realizes that braving the dangers of the open sea is the only way to survive. Pauli finds courage as the waves beat against the flimsy boat and the sun beats down on their unprotected bodies. The final challenge comes with the capsizing of their boat. They must swim to survive, and some will not make it.

Novel

📖 *Monkey Island* by Paula Fox. New York: Orchard Books, 1991.

Clay, 11 years old, sleeps in a big park in New York City. It is the safest place he can find now that his parents have left him. In need of companionship, he finds young homeless men who sleep in the park. Clay is always hungry, fearful, and desperate to find his mother. He witnesses daily brutality. There are harsh days and terrifying nights, but some acts of kindness give Clay a glimmer of hope. After becoming sick, Clay is taken to a hospital where people from Social Services help him find his mother. He realizes that his mother abandoned him in a desperate move to save her unborn baby. Clay finds joy in her happiness at his return and in the smile of his new baby sister.

Magic

Connection: Finding Magic

Picture Book

📖 *Nobody Rides the Unicorn* by Adrian Mitchell. Illustrated by Stephan Lambert. New York: Arthur A. Levine Books, 1999.

The King of Joppardy believes that only a unicorn can save his life. He is told that only a sweet, quiet girl with a lovely song can capture a unicorn. Everyone in the kingdom knows that only the beggar girl, Zoe, fits this description. The king orders Zoe to capture the unicorn and she agrees, not knowing that the unicorn is to be killed. When Zoe learns the truth, she sets the unicorn free. She has no home, friends, or family, but still she frees the beautiful beast. Zoe, a "little nobody," is banished and roams the kingdom knowing that her only hope is in finding the land of the unicorns. When she finally finds it, she sings her lovely song and learns that by becoming "Nobody" she alone can ride the unicorn.

Discussion

1. What magical powers did medieval people believe the unicorn possessed?

2. What sea animal has a horn much like the unicorn's?

3. Name some other mythical animals from medieval times.

Novel

📖 *Into the Land of the Unicorns* by Bruce Coville. New York: Scholastic, 1994.

Cara loves and trusts her grandmother enough to risk death to follow Grandmother's instructions. However, when it is time to throw herself from the church tower to escape the terror that followed her up the many steps, she hesitates. She hopes death will not meet her and is overjoyed to discover the land of the unicorns instead. In this land called Luster, Cara meets many strange creatures, in addition to the wonderful and mighty unicorns. She is destined to save these unicorns, if only she can reach the Queen. Cara faces danger and terror during her journey and harbors many unanswered questions about her grandmother's role in the magical land of Luster. The biggest question concerns the identity of the man chasing her up the church tower steps. Some of the questions are answered at the court of the Queen at Summerhaven—and some will be answered in the sequel.

Novel

The Transfigured Hart by Jane Yolen. Illustrated by Donna Diamond. New York: Thomas Y. Crowell, 1975.

Richard, aged 12, sees a magnificent white hart one autumn day and knows that he must save it from the hunters before deer hunting season begins. He dreams of taming the animal, keeping it for himself. However, Heather has also seen the animal, and she has similar ideas. The white hart was different from the time of birth and grew up to be a loner—very much like Richard. Heather, on the other hand, is an extrovert and a joiner. These two unlikely people band together to save the beautiful albino hart. Richard is the first to realize that the hart is a unicorn. Heather insists that unicorns are imaginary. But how else can one explain its lack of antlers and its whiteness? The two travel to the blue, magical pool of the unicorn to confirm their beliefs. They stay through the night with the gentle beast and in the morning find the way to save it from the hunters' guns.

Mind Control

Connection: Fighting Those Who Control

Picture Book

📖 *The Watertower* by Gary Crew. Illustrated by Steven Woolman. New York: Crocodile Books U.S.A., 1999.

Swimming in the water tower on a blistering hot day is an irresistible temptation for two boys, Spike and Bubba. The old and rusty tower stands dark and slightly menacing on the edge of town. The metal posts and barbed wire of last year's security fence lie twisted and flattened to the ground. The boys don't stop to wonder about the fence as they climb inside to slip into the murky, swirling water. Bubba begins to feel uneasy and leaves the water first. However, when he climbs out of the tank he discovers that his pants are missing. Fearing his mother's wrath, he lets Spike run home to sneak him another pair. Left alone, Bubba returns to the tank to escape the dreadful heat. The tank and swirling water seem eerie to him, and he goes back outside. After climbing down from the top he manages to find some bushes to hide under and watches the tall tank in front of him. As he watches, he sees some dreadful thing at the top of the tank! When Spike returns he finds Bubba back in the tank and changed in a very mysterious way.

Discussion

1. Name some unexplained and unusual phenomena in this world.

2. Do you think it is possible to control someone's mind? Why or why not?

3. Debate the positive and negative aspects of mind control.

Novel

📖 *A Dusk of Demons* by John Christopher. New York: Macmillan, 1994.

Ben lives an enjoyable and quiet life on Old Isle, away from the mainland, until the Master's death. He knows that the family he had known from as far back as memory served him are not his own, but he does not know that he is the Master's son. Old Isle now belongs to him and he faces the horrifying task of defending it against the demons, a task that seems beyond his powers. The demons burn the family home and force most of the family to flee to the mainland. Ben remains to struggle against the evil forces, only to find himself a prisoner. He escapes from the Isle with the help of a faithful friend, Paddy. However, the mainland reveals more terror as Ben faces the gloom and the cries of those condemned to the demons.

Novel

📖 *The Giver* by Lois Lowry. Boston: Houghton Mifflin, 1993.

Jonas lives the perfect life, one with no pain, poverty, divorce, unemployment, or inequality. However, he becomes uneasy about his approaching life assignment, given at a yearly ceremony when a child reaches the age of 12. His friend Fiona is good with older people, so she is selected as Caretaker of the Old. His fun-loving buddy Asher will be Assistant Director of Recreation. Jonas's assignment is to study under someone called the Giver to eventually become the Receiver of Memories. Through his sessions with the Giver, Jonas discovers the disturbing truth about their so-called ideal world and why no one feels pain, frustration, or need. Jonas realizes that without such realities, one cannot truly know happiness or fulfillment. He chooses to sacrifice whatever is necessary to escape to another world, an escape that will be overwhelmingly painful.

Novel

📖 *Others See Us* by William Sleator. New York: E. P. Dutton, 1993.

Jared looks forward to a wonderful summer vacation with his attractive cousin, Annilise. He is enjoying the visit at his grandmother's house until he falls into a swamp filled with toxic waste. Everything in his life changes with the realization that he can now read minds. The first thing he uncovers is a heinous crime committed by his cousin, the beautiful but evil Annilise. Jared realizes that he must protect the family from her. To make matters worse he finds out that his grandmother also has mind-reading powers, and there is a terrible struggle of wills among the three of them. Jared cannot escape either the voices in his head or the obligation to his family. He gains more mind-reading power through drinking additional swampy water, but his grandmother has drunk more than any of them. As events become more dangerous, Jared is saved by Annilise's revelations through her journal about the evil person that she has become. The family realizes Annilese's true nature, but what will the grandmother's next move be? How will her mind-reading power influence the rest of the family?

Miracles

Connection: Experiencing Miracles

Picture Book

📖 *The Acrobat and the Angel* by Mark Shannon. Illustrated by David Shannon. New York: G. P. Putnam's Sons, 1999.

Pequele's life during the Middle Ages is harsh and difficult. Having lost both parents to the black plague, he lives with his grandmother in abject poverty. But Pequele has an angel to hold onto. His mother had made it for him of branches and dried flowers. She tucked it in his shirt before she died, and the angel guided him in many ways. When things look hopeless after Grandmother dies, Pequele is led to the monastery where the monks care for him and marvel at his acrobatic abilities. The boy can leap and tumble like no other they have ever seen. Pequele uses his talents to bring some joy into the lives of the peasant people. In doing so he comes into contact with the dreaded plague. Only the angel can come to his rescue and when she does, miracles happen.

Discussion

1. How would you define a miracle?

2. The plague and many other hardships were a part of medieval life. Why do you think miracles were an important part of these people's beliefs?

3. Can you think of any modern miracles?

Novel

The Christmas Box by Richard Paul Evans. New York: Simon & Schuster, 1998.

A young couple and their four-year-old daughter move into a mansion with an elderly lady, Mary, who needs help with her yard and food preparation. It becomes clear that she needs companionship more than anything else. The preparations for Christmas bond them together quickly. Mary loves the family and they learn about the sadness that guides her life. The Christmas box in the attic and the music that flows from it seem to be miraculous. The letters inside add to the mystery and lead to an angel in the cemetery that reveals Mary's sorrow. Mary dies on Christmas day, but her death is joyful. The Christmas box remains a treasured reminder of the true meaning of life.

Novel

The Trees Kneel at Christmas by Maud Hart Lovelace. Illustrated by Marie-Claude Monchaux. Edina, MN: ABDO & Daughters, 1951.

Grandmother knows that there is a miracle performed every Christmas. On Christmas Eve, Grandmother tells her two grandchildren about the trees that kneel in her homeland of Lebanon, explaining that only people of great faith see this miracle. She assures them that no one in Brooklyn will see the trees that kneel because their faith is not strong enough. Hanna and her brother believe that they have enough faith to see the kneeling trees. They decide to visit Prospect Park at midnight to see the miracle. All day the children help their mother and grandmother with the cleaning and cooking for Christmas Day. All day they think of nothing but their trip to the park. At midnight the faith of the little children leads them to the miracle of the kneeling trees.

Native American Identity

Connection: Preserving Identity

Picture Book

📖 *Cheyenne Again* by Eve Bunting. Illustrated by Irving Toddy. New York: Clarion Books, 1995.

Young Bull is forced to leave his family, his home, and his friends. The whites take away his clothing, his freedom, his language—even his religion. In exchange, Young Bull is schooled in white ways and culture in a boarding school far away from home. He is expected to be grateful. Instead, Young Bull cries for home and runs away on a dark and snowy night. Trackers find him and fasten him to a ball and chain. Life in the white world is dismal and without hope for the Indian boy until he meets one teacher who understands and encourages him to keep his memories of being Indian. Young Bull finds comfort in drawing pictures of his past life and in remembering the times on the golden plains and in his dreams of becoming Cheyenne again.

Discussion

1. Why do you think many Indian children were forced to attend white schools in the 1880s?

2. Do you consider such actions to be morally correct?

3. How are the boarding schools for Native American children today different from those of a hundred years ago?

Novel

📖 *A Woman of Her Tribe* by Margaret A. Robinson. New York: Charles Scribner's Sons, 1990.

Annette is forced to live in two very different worlds: the world of the Indian and the world of the whites. Her mother feels strongly that Annette needs to know about her English heritage as well as the Indian ways she has experienced up to this time. Annette's Indian grandmother does not trust the white culture and the influence it will have on her granddaughter. This feeling is passed on to the girl. Regardless of her feelings, Annette knows she is going to a Canadian private school where she will encounter many strange and confusing experiences. Everything in the white world is different from her father's village where she grew up with the Nootka Indians. The lonely girl is without much hope for happiness in her new surroundings until she begins to make new friends, including a boyfriend. When Annette finally returns to her Indian world she realizes the change in herself and begins to wonder if she will ever find a world where she truly belongs.

Novel

📖 *The Rainmakers* by E. J. Bird. Minneapolis, MN: Carolrhoda Books, 1993.

In his eleventh summer, Cricket, an Anasazi Indian, enjoys his life in a village of rock and clay set in the sheer cliffs above a canyon. It is a lively and safe place surrounded by beautiful countryside. The cave homes are almost hidden in the canyon and are protected from weather and raiding Plains tribes of Indians. Cricket loves his home and people, and he enjoys playing music on his flute and trading with the other tribes. He loves to listen to the stories told by Grandfather and to join in the many tribal celebrations. But nothing can compare to this summer when he finds the small orphaned black bear. The village is part of the Bear Clan, and Cricket is allowed to keep the bear. Cricket, his best friend, Sheep, and the bear embark on many adventures: A girl called Little Snowflower is kidnapped and needs to be rescued; there is a wild ride down the river; and a wounded bison bull charges Grandfather. But the two boys and their bear save the day. The villagers find their very survival depending on the three.

Perception

Connection: Different Perceptions

Picture Book

Switch on the Night by Ray Bradbury. Illustrated by Leo Dillon and Diane Dillon. New York: Alfred A. Knopf, 2000.

In this original fable, a boy fears the night. He likes "lanterns and lamps, torches and tapers, beacons and bonfires, flashlights and flares." In fact, he likes any kind of light. When night comes, his room is the only one with a light on in the whole town. Because he refuses to step outside after dark, he can only listen as other children play on the night lawn. Lost in his lonely thoughts, he is astonished to discover he has a night visitor, a small girl named Dark. "When you switch on the night," she says, "You switch on crickets and frogs, and stars and the great white moon." She shows him exactly how to do it. The boy is ecstatic. He had no idea that it was possible to switch on the night. Now he has a night switch instead of a light switch. The illustrators dedicate this book to M. C. Escher because their mysterious and haunting illustrations evoke some of the fascinating perspectives of this famous artist.

Discussion

1. Explain this statement: *Perception equals value equals action.*

2. What causes two people to react differently to the same situation?

3. Why do eyewitnesses to an event often differ in their descriptions of the event?

Novel

📖 *Nothing But the Truth: A Documentary Novel* by Avi. New York: Orchard Books, 1991.

Philip, an angry ninth grader, cannot be on the track team due to a poor English grade. One morning he angers his English teacher by humming along as the "Star Spangled Banner" is played. Students are expected to stand at "silent, respectful attention," and the ensuing confrontation results in a two-day suspension. The media become involved and play up the mistaken idea that Philip is not being allowed to express his patriotism as he wishes. The entire community becomes involved. Some perceive the situation as unfair to the boy, others let preconceptions get in the way of the truth, and still others generate misinformation. Simply put, the characters behave the way they do because they see the same incidents in very different ways. Further, everyone believes they are telling "nothing but the truth." In the end, nobody wins. Philip transfers to another school without a track team and the English teacher is forced to take a leave. The surprise ending further reveals the needlessness of the conflict.

Connection: Different Perspectives

Picture Book

📖 *From a Distance* by Julie Gold. Illustrated by Jane Ray Dutton. New York: E. P. Dutton, 1998.

From a distance all things look different. Sometimes stepping back provides a clearer perspective on things that are important to us. This song and picture book does exactly that by providing the reader with a bird's-eye view of our world. From a distance the colors are vivid, the mountains are majestic, and the waterways show their maze of connections. The land is lush and green, and all looks peaceful and well ordered. There is music all around and there is unity among people. There is no war, no hatred, and no poverty. Then the reader sees the world from a close-up view and discovers the attacking planes, the poor, the hungry, and people of different faiths being persecuted. Only from a distance can readers see the world as God sees it and as He intended it to be.

Discussion

1. What is the difference between subjective and objective approaches to an issue?

2. Why do you think it is important to occasionally look at things from a distance?

3. What do we mean by "point of view?"

Novel

📖 *Fly Free* by C. S. Adler. New York: Coward-McCann, 1984.

Shari, at age 13, has to find ways to step back from her problems to be able to deal with them. Shari's mother is abusive and cruel, and Shari cannot understand why her mother does not give her the kindness and understanding her brothers receive. Shari does get love from her father and her little brother, but she is a shy girl and finds it difficult to make new friends. She retreats from her world when it becomes too much to bear and finds happiness in tramping through the woods and watching the birds. She can imagine herself soaring and gliding above the Earth where no earthly thing can touch her. These defenses serve Shari well until she nearly loses the one thing in the world she cannot live without. Then her mother reveals the hurtful truth of who Shari really is. She has to find an escape and the opportunity comes just in time. Shari finds a way to "fly free."

Novel

📖 *The Door in the Lake* by Nancy Butts. Chicago: Front Street, 1998.

Coming back to Earth after two years is a fearful and inexplicable thing for 14-year-old Joey. It is bad enough to have lost two years of his life, but where did those two years go, and why does he look exactly as he did when he disappeared on the family camping trip? Joey tries to understand all the strange things happening to him as he comes slowly back to his world, but there are few answers to the hundreds of questions in his mind. Why is his nose always running? What are the voices in his head, and why doesn't he want to remember the smell of the burning light? Joey is glad to see his family and his dog again. But his friends all look different, whereas nothing physical has changed about Joey. Joey's answers come from two college students who know something about aliens and from the voice in his head that convinces him to return to the door in the lake. He will have to look at his world from another perspective.

The Pioneer Spirit

Connection: Pioneer Life

Picture Book

📖 *Dakota Dugout* by Ann Turner. Illustrated by Ronald Himler. New York: Macmillan, 1985.

One hundred years ago, a courageous woman boards a train in the city to travel across the country to join her husband on the prairie. She is shocked when she views her first home. a sod house built into the side of a mound. But she accepts the challenges and tries to create a home. Snakes drop on her bed at night during the summer, and winter winds blow through the cracks of the hut. When the summer crop that promises a better life for the couple fails, they face bitter disappointment. Then despair settles in when 12 of their herd of cattle die in a winter storm. As the woman talks to the sparrows, the reader understands the realities of her lonely life. Finally, life improves, and the couple manage to build a modern clapboard house. In spite of their new, comfortable surroundings, the woman fondly recalls that first prairie home.

Discussion

1. Why will people leave the comfortable and familiar to venture into unknown and sometimes dangerous situations?

2. Why might one wish for a return to harder times when life becomes more comfortable?

3. Is it possible to be a pioneer today? How?

Novel

Grasshopper Summer by Ann Turner. New York: Macmillan, 1989.

Sam White likes Kentucky. He likes fishing and joking with his friends, the cool shade under the trees in summer, his grandmother's peach pies, and his grandfather's soldierly ways. But Sam's father is restless, still haunted by the bloodshed of the Civil War. He resolves to make a new life for himself and his family in the Dakota Territory. Sam can't stand the idea of leaving behind his grandparents and the orderly, familiar life of their farm. But his father wants the land offered by the government that will be theirs as long as they plant 10 acres, build a house, and stay for five years. The journey west is long and difficult, and when the White family finally reach the Dakotas, things are tougher still. To Sam the sod house they are building feels like a grave, and the endless prairie sky empty and unwelcoming. But he does his best to stop missing Kentucky and begins to look forward to their first harvest. Then the grasshoppers come, eating every green thing in sight.

Novel

📖 *Bluestem* by Frances Arrington. New York: Philomel Books, 2000.

When Polly and Jessie come back to their prairie soddy and discover Mama just sitting there, rocking and not saying anything, they know it has something to do with her losing the baby in the winter. They know Papa is not coming back soon enough from his brother's farm to help them. But, sure as they're alive and the prairie is blue, they also know they need to keep going—for Mama, for Papa, and for themselves—despite their meddling neighbors. In this heroic story, set on the open prairie in the 1870s, two young sisters, armed only with love for each other, face a new world alone.

The Power of Nature

Connection: Appreciating Nature

Picture Book

📖 *The Bird House* by Cynthia Rylant. New York: E. P. Dutton, 1998.

A young girl with neither home nor family wanders alone in the woods. She "had been sad for a very long time." Then she spies a small cottage and sees a variety of birds greet the old woman who lives there. One in particular, the Great Bared Owl, hovers above the door, ever watchful. The girl is afraid to approach the cottage but her fascination with the birds draws her closer to them. The birds rise into the sky and spell the word GIRL. She is frightened but returns the following day and finds herself caught and held by the Great Owl. The old woman, hearing her cries, takes her into the cottage, where they talk through the night. The girl becomes a part of this small family and loses her fears as she greets the birds each day. This haunting tale leaves the reader with as many questions as answers. Who is the girl? Where had she come from? Why is she alone? Why is she sad? What are the metaphors in the tale?

Discussion

1. List ways in which humans are affected physically by nature.

2. List ways in which humans are affected mentally by nature.

3. In what ways can nature heal?

Novel

📖 *Going Through the Gate* by Janet S. Anderson. New York: E. P. Dutton, 1997.

    Imagine a small rural town where almost no one eats meat and cats rarely hunt. The graduation ceremony for five sixth graders in the one-room school is one most parents have been through but do not talk about. Preceding the ceremony, each child collaborates with the teacher, Miss Clough, to choose an animal to study. It becomes clear that the chosen animal reflects the children's concerns about approaching adulthood. Becky, a middle child, relates to the chickadee. Mary Margaret, from a large, quarrelsome family, finds hope and peace in the swallow. Penny relates to the colorful cardinal. Eddie loves frogs, and Tim relates to the freedom of the trout. As the ceremony progresses, the children "go through the gate," an experience that transforms each into an animal for a short time. These children learn to treasure the natural world and discover things about themselves that they had not previously realized.

Connection: Facing Danger

Picture Book

📖 *River of Life* by Debbie S. Miller. Illustrated by Jon Van Zyle. New York: Clarion Books, 2000.

Fish and insects, bears and birds, plants and humans all depend on the river for their existence. Water is life. The life of the river begins with the winter's sparkling snow and ice lying thick on an Alaskan mountaintop. With spring comes the great melt and the beginning of the water's journey down the mountainside where it will nourish the trees and provide homes for fish and insects. The water, now a river, provides food for birds and drink for all living nearby. By summer the salmon swim upriver to spawn where they may serve as food for eagles, bears, and humans. Even the sediment from the river harbors worms and ants, while wildflowers bloom in the rich soil and drop their tiny seeds for the squirrels in autumn. Winter returns and the cycle of life begins again in the high, cold places of the mountain. The people and animals of Alaska rejoice in their 3,000 life-giving rivers.

Discussion

1. What are the names of the major rivers in the state you live in? What impact does a river have on your community?

2. What is the longest river in the world? The largest?

3. Why are some rivers dammed to provide reservoirs? What are the pros and cons of this practice?

Novel

River Runners by James Huston. New York: Atheneum, 1979.

Not many 15-year-old boys live under constant life-and-death circumstances. Andrew lives in the Artic regions, where life is hard and dangerous. The cold is deadly and the ice creates many dangers on the land as well as on the river used for transportation. Andrew thinks he understands the hardships and courage needed to live in this frozen land, but its true harshness is revealed when he and an Indian boy, Pashak, are sent deep into the northern regions of Canada to set up a fur-trading outpost. They leave in late autumn when they can follow the frozen river on snowshoes and sleds. The boys face wolves and a brutally cold winter. The stinging cold takes their breath as they struggle up the frozen river toward the Naskapi Indian village. Andrew knows that he could never survive without Pashak. There are many ways to die in this unforgiving land. The boys reach the Naskapi people living along the treacherous rivers in the northern Arctic land and discover a new enemy: starvation. The caribou have failed to appear this winter, and people have little food. Can Andrew and Pashak find a way on the river to save themselves and the others?

Novel

📖 *River Danger* by Thomas J. Dygard. New York: Morrow Junior Books, 1998.

Canoeing down the Buffalo River is one of Eric's greatest thrills. He knows the river and delights in leaving the world behind, escaping down the watery pathways with his younger brother, Robbie. They had planned to take their trip before the big canoe season begins so that they can spend five or six days enjoying the freedom, the campsites, and the wonderful views of the surrounding woods. All goes well until Eric and Robbie are separated. Eric searches for Robbie in the woods, and instead of finding Robbie, he finds two criminals involved in a car theft ring. They capture Eric, who bravely tries to find a way out. Robbie discovers his brother's dilemma and realizes that only he can save him. Can he get help in time?

Connection: Coping with Winter

Picture Book

📖 *The Silver Swan* by Michael Morpurgo. Illustrated by Christine Birmingham. New York: Phyllis Fogelman Books, 2000.

Great love stories are sometimes found in unusual places. This love story takes place on a northern lake and unfolds before the eyes of a young boy. The lovers are a pair of beautiful white swans who meet and mate. They then swim and fly together "with wings that beat as one." The boy watches in fascination as they try to survive the unusually harsh winter while building their nest to house the cygnets who will soon arrive. Their actions demonstrate their devotion to each other and to the five new members of the family. As the boy watches, all goes well until the winter drags on too long, and a starving fox searches for a meal to save her own kits. All the love that the boy and the swan cob have for the silver swan cannot save her from the harshness of nature. The boy is devastated when he hears the swan's song of death. The cob then loses his will to live without his mate. Can nature provide hope and comfort as well as despair and pain?

Discussion

1. Name an animal other than the swan that mates for life.

2. What are some important lessons we can learn from animals?

3. What sacrifices might your parents make if you were starving?

Novel

📖 *Tracks in the Snow* by Lucy Jane Bledsoe. New York: Holiday House, 1997.

Erin is a good and loyal friend. She refuses to listen to her teacher and her mother's advice when her babysitter, Amy, doesn't show up on a cold, gray morning. Erin knows that something is terribly wrong. Amy may dress and act differently, but that doesn't mean she is irresponsible. Erin decides to enlist the help of another friend, Tiffany, to find out what happened to Amy. They use an animal track project as an excuse to set off through the woods. The girls do not plan on fighting a spring blizzard, a twisted ankle, and wild animals. Soon they, like the wild animals, are fighting for survival.

Novel

📖 *The Sign of the Beaver* by Elizabeth George Speare. Boston: Houghton Mifflin, 1983.

No 13-year-old boy of today can imagine how it would feel to be left all alone in the early American wilderness surrounded by Indians and wild animals. Matt's father leaves him in charge of their cabin while he returns to their old home to pick up the rest of the family. The loneliness and the quiet are the hardest to bear at first. Then things get worse when Matt's gun is stolen, and a bear gets all his food. Fish from the river will be his only food. He almost loses his fight for survival when he tries to get honey from a bee tree. The Indian who saves Matt strikes a bargain, and Matt begins to teach the Indian's grandson, Attean, how to read. The boys form a strong bond and learn from each other. Matt also learns to respect the Indians, facing a difficult choice when the tribe moves and asks Matt to join them. Will Matt continue to wait far beyond the expected arrival of his family or leave with his new friends?

The Price of Freedom

Connection: Those in Bondage

Picture Book

📖 *The Wagon* by Tony Johnston. Illustrated by James E. Ransome. New York: Tambourine Books, 1996.

On a Carolina morning a child is born into slavery. Soon he is working for the master from dawn to dark. As he grows, he dreams that the wagon he has helped build for the master is a glorious chariot to freedom. The boy becomes angry and defiant, and his back feels the whip when his anger shows once too often. One night he dreams about chopping wood with President Lincoln. Finally the boy's dream of freedom becomes reality. When the master asks the boy's father if there is anything he wants, the father replies, "the wagon." This is a brutal look at slavery and a poignant account of a young boy's dream of freedom.

Picture Book

📖 *Barefoot: Escape on the Underground Railroad* by Pamela Duncan Edwards. Illustrated by Henry Cole. New York: HarperCollins, 1997.

Under cover of darkness, a Barefoot, an escaped slave, flees for his life. He is terrified, and he sees no signs of the Underground Railroad, his road to freedom, because the clouds hide the moon. Then a frog croaks, leading the Barefoot to water. A mouse rustles where berries grow, and the Barefoot eats. When the Barefoot's captors close in, a heron cries, warning of danger. With the creatures of the night to guide him, the Barefoot finds a safe haven.

Discussion

1. Cite instances throughout history when people have risked their lives for personal freedom.

2. Why do you think it is possible for a few people to control the personal freedom of many?

3. Could the tale of Barefoot actually have happened? Why or why not?

4. How are education and personal freedom connected?

Novel

📖 *Nightjohn* by Gary Paulsen. New York: Delacorte Press, 1983.

"To know things, for us to know things, is bad for them. We get to wanting and when we get to wanting it's bad for them. . . . That's why they don't want us reading."—Nightjohn. "I didn't know what letters was, nor what they meant, but I thought it might be something I wanted to know. To learn."—Sarny. Sarny, a female slave at the Waller plantation, first sees Nightjohn when he is brought there with a rope around his neck, his body covered in scars. He had escaped north to freedom, but he came back. Knowing that the penalty for reading is dismemberment,

Nightjohn still returns to teach the slaves how to read. And 12-year-old Sarny is willing to take the risk to learn.

Novel

📖 *Letters from a Slave Girl: The Story of Harriet Jacobs* by Mary E. Lyons. New York: Charles Scribner's Sons, 1992.

Harriet Jacobs has lived her entire life in slavery. Daughter and granddaughter of slaves in North Carolina, she knows no other existence. In 1825, with the death of Margaret Horniblow, the motherly mistress who has taught young Harriet to read, there is hope that Miss Horniblow's will provides for Harriet's freedom. Crushed to find that the will has merely transferred control of Harriet to Margaret Horniblow's sister and her menacing husband, Harriet sees escape to freedom in the North as her only option. Numerous ordeals face her before she experiences that glorious moment. Through Harriet's riveting letters the reader shares her fears, struggles, and dreams. *Letters from a Slave Girl* reveals in poignant detail what thousands of African-American women endured in the United States little more than a century ago.

Novel

📖 *Dear Austin* by Elvira Woodruff. New York: Alfred A. Knopf, 1998.

Levi Ives dreams of joining his brother, Austin, who has escaped to the West where the family is determined to make a new home. For now he recuperates from consumption in Pennsylvania in the year 1853 and finds danger and adventure that few 11-year-olds face. Levi communicates with Austin through letters, and we see calamity coming when he writes about the slave catchers who constantly search for runaway slaves. They touch his life when his friend Jupiter's sister is taken and disappears into the deep South. Levi and Jupiter prepare to travel south to rescue her. It will be a dangerous trip, but the boys know what they have to do. We follow their trip through Levi's letters to Austin as the boys encounter hunger and dangerous animals and lose their way. The trip is a nightmare, but they do find help from the Underground

Railroad. When Jupiter is caught and taken to the slave auction, only a miracle can save him.

Problems of Society

Connection: Resisting Drugs

Picture Book

📖 *The House That Crack Built* by Clark Taylor. Illustrated by Jan Thompson Dicks. San Francisco: Chronicle Books, 1992.

This book of few words teaches that drugs are for losers. Patterned on "The House That Jack Built," it is a refrain of hopelessness, pain, and death. This sad and discouraging story, acted out on the streets every day, never changes. Those who provide the drugs make fortunes from selling them to desperate and despairing people who are hooked on cocaine. The victims include the inner-city kids who use crack as their escape from drab and hopeless lives as well as the growers of the plant who have no other means of survival. Other victims include the gangs who rule the streets and abuse their power, but who also live in fear, and the police who fight the use of drugs while knowing they are engaged in a losing battle. The saddest victims are the crack babies born to the addicted mothers.

Picture Book

📖 *The Inner City Mother Goose* by Eve Merriam. Illustrated by David Diaz. New York: Simon & Schuster, 1982.

These Mother Goose rhymes reflect the desperation, suffering, neglect, and danger found in many inner city areas. In these simple rhymes readers recognize those without hope and dreams and with little support from the system. The verses expose the overwhelming problems of poverty, drugs, moral decay, and dangerous weapons. Readers feel

the sad rhythms of men without work, children who have lost their inno-
cence, and disintegrating family life. These simple rhymes are a cry for
help and for solutions.

Discussion

1. Why are we all victims of the drug problem, whether we use drugs
    or not?

2. Do you agree with those who say that legalization of drug use
    would solve the problem? Why or why not?

3. What are some problems associated with legalized drugs?

Novel

📖 *Fast Sam, Cool Clyde and Stuff* by Walter Dean Myers. New
York: Viking, 1975.

It isn't easy growing up and getting through the teen years for any
kid or in any neighborhood. Doing it successfully is even more challenging in the inner-city of New York. There you find danger of many
kinds on every street corner.

Francis moved into this type of neighborhood with his family and
hoped to survive. He knew that a lot depended on who his friends turned
out to be. Francis got lucky; his first contacts were with Fast Sam, Cool
Clyde, and Gloria. They thought he was a hotshot basketball player, so
they renamed him Stuff. Francis liked his new name and his new friends.

The next year was filled with growing-up experiences for all of
them. They formed a club in the neighborhood for protection from dangerous gangs, drug pushers, and lethal weapons. During that year Stuff
found out about death and fell in love for the first time. He also discovered the value of friendship.

There were difficult choices to be made when the parties they went
to involved alcohol and drugs. Stuff was fortunate to have parents who
made their ideas on substance abuse very clear. However, the strongest
deterrent against drugs was learning what happened to Carnation
Chaday!

Connection: Fighting Drugs

Picture Book

📖 *Riding the Tiger* by Eve Bunting. New York: Clarion Books, 2001.

Danny is proud when the tiger first comes for him. He climbs up on its back and together they cruise the neighborhood. Shopkeepers and passersby give them respect. Danny feels powerful and much older than 10. Soon, though, Danny realizes it isn't respect the people feel for him and the tiger, it is fear. And when he wants to get down off the tiger's back it isn't so easy. This allegorical fantasy carries a powerful message about temptation, conformity, and the loss of control that comes when you ride any kind of tiger.

Discussion

1. What do you think is the message of this story? Is the author's presentation effective in getting the message across?

2. What do you think are the most pressing problems of the inner city? Can you think of possible solutions for them?

3. Why do you think it is important to address the problems of inner cities?

Novel

📖 *Go Ask Alice* by Anonymous. New York: Avon Books, 1967.

This is the diary of a girl who is desperate because she has lost control of her life. She tries to convince herself she can leave the drugs whenever she wants, yet she knows the horrible reality of her complete addiction. She is 15 years old and fears she is losing her mind. She prays to God for help but always returns to the drugs. Alice swings from elation to utter dejection in a matter of hours. She cares for her boyfriend, Roger, and yearns for his attention. She is crushed when it isn't given.

When the family decides to move, Alice is happy for awhile and school becomes more exciting. Life is better, but the old feelings of loneliness and isolation return with a vengeance. Her moods fit her weight—up and down. She turns to drugs again and lives the doper's life, one without hope. She leaves her family, her only support. Redemption from the horror of Alice's existence seems possible when she returns home, but over time the need for drugs pulls her back into the abyss. Alice writes about her love life, her dreams, her family, and her happier moments. Will she conquer the demon?

Novel

📖 *Breaking the Ring* by Donna Walsh Inglehart. Boston: Little, Brown, 1991.

Summer fun is all Jesse thinks of as she and her sister travel to the beautiful St. Lawrence River and the islands for their vacation. Jesse is 15 and is looking for adventure. She thinks she has found it when she and her best friend, Maggie, hear about the ghost that haunts one of the islands. The girls investigate and find much more than they had bargained for. It isn't a ghost island; it is a drug dealers' island, and the smugglers know they have been found out.

Connection: The Inner City

Picture Book

📖 *Smoky Night* by Eve Bunting. Illustrated by David Diaz. New York: Voyager Books, 1994.

Daniel and his mother spend a terrifying night in their apartment when neighborhood thugs decide to burn and destroy everything on the block. Daniel realizes that Mama is doing everything she can to protect them from being killed, but the fear is overwhelming. There are the fires, the bullets, and the looters who smash or burn and take whatever they want from the buildings and stores. There are so many ways to get hurt or to die. But Daniel's main fear is for his pet cat, Jasmine, who flees when the apartment is set afire. Along with their neighbors, Daniel and his mother hurry to the shelter. The shelter is full of crying and frightened people, but it's there that Daniel is reunited with Jasmine. Two rescued cats show the people of the neighborhood that they must learn to live together in understanding and harmony if there is to be any hope for peace among them.

Discussion

1. What is bias and prejudice?

2. Why do you think there is prejudice?

3. What can you do to alleviate prejudice?

Novel

The $66 Summer by John Armistead. Minneapolis, MN: Milkweed Editions, 2000.

In 1955, George moves south for the summer to live with his grandmother, wanting to make money for a motorcycle. He faces racism that he has never known before. George is white and his summer friends, Esther and Bennett, are black. Bennett is a great fisherman and works for a mean man who raises fighting dogs. Esther is determined to raise money for her education. Esther and Bennett often wonder what happened to their father, who has been missing for four years. George wonders about this mystery too, but it doesn't stop the three from having many exciting times together. The summer becomes ominous when the threesome discovers the hooded one, who follows them through the woods. The secret unravels about Esther and Bennett's father. Prejudice is an ugly thing for George to face, but he also finds beauty in tolerance.

Novel

📖 *Circle of Fire* by William Hooks. New York: Atheneum, 1983.

Harrison Hawkins is a white boy living in the south during the 1930s. He is only 11 years old, but he knows all about bigotry and narrow-mindedness. His two best friends are a black boy named Kitty and his sister, called Scrap. Harrison can't understand why grown-ups don't get along like kids do. He intends to be friends with Kitty and Scrap forever, but he faces significant odds with all the prejudice surrounding them. All three of the friends get a lesson in this evil when they come into contact with some Irish tinkers. Most people call them gypsies and have little use for them. The tinkers camp in a hollow near town, and it isn't long before the townspeople plan to run them out of the area. Harrison knows the tinkers are camping on his family's land. He also knows that they had to flee from the Ku Klux Klan and that being called "gypsy" is an insult. Harrison uncovers the Klan's plan to attack the tinker camp on Christmas day. He wants to prevent the attack, but he overhears a conversation his father has with a possible Klan member. He is overwhelmed with fear and doubt, but with the help of Kitty, Christmas turns out as happy as it should be.

Connection: The Great Depression

Picture Book

📖 *Tree of Hope* by Amy Littlesugar. Illustrated by Floyd Cooper. New York: Philomel Books, 1999.

The Harlem Renaissance was a glorious time for the black people who loved theater and for black writers, poets, and artists. Life was good in the 1920s. However, the 1930s bring the Great Depression and a fight for survival. Florrie's family lives in Harlem. Daddy has to give up his dreams of the theater to take a job at a bakery. Mom also has to work long hours, and life is grim. But Florrie has a dream and she makes a wish on the tree of hope. She wants Daddy to be back on the stage and for life to be a little less bleak for everyone. Then President Roosevelt decides that the theater should be reopened for plays and entertainment.

Orson Welles produces and directs *Macbeth*. Florrie is overwhelmed with hope that there will be a part in the play for her dad. However, this is a play for white people. How could her father fit in? Florrie and Mom are almost afraid to hope. Daddy has always believed in the tree of hope, and the wish is made.

Discussion

1. When it was so hard just to get the basic necessities of life during the Great Depression, why do you think President F. D. Roosevelt decided the theater opening was important?

2. Do you see any connection between this and the rulers of Rome providing free entertainment for the masses of the Roman empire?

3. What does the word "Renaissance" mean?

4. If an African-American *Macbeth* were staged today, what leading actors would you choose for the good King? Macbeth? His greedy and selfish wife?

Novel

📖 *Treasures in the Dust* by Tracey Porter. New York: Joanne Cotler Books, 1997.

Annie Mae and Violet are the best of friends, and that is the one thing that makes life bearable while living on their dusty, barren land during the Great Depression. The times are difficult, with little work for men and too many funerals to attend. Life is often a matter of bare survival. The girls are different in many ways. One is a realist who loves to search for fossils; the other is a dreamer who hopes to be a movie star. Still, they support each other in their harsh world of dust storms and drought when money is scarce and poverty is prevalent. Violet must quit school and go to work. Violet and Annie Mae face hardship and bitter decisions, but they find comfort and courage in their enduring friendship.

Novel

📖 *Dave at Night* by Gail Carson Levine. New York: HarperCollins, 1999.

"Home," the Hebrew Home for Boys in the lower east side of New York City, is a strange name for the place where Dave finds himself after his father dies. Deciding to stay until he can find another place, Dave determines to take care of himself. However, he learns how harsh life can be during the Great Depression. People are desperate and the Home provides no real haven. There are strict rules, tasteless food, and constant danger from the other inhabitants, who are both cruel and stronger than he. The greatest threat to Dave is Mr. Doom, who runs the school and enjoys using the yardstick or his fists to "teach the boys a lesson." Dave discovers the saloons in the Harlem area, escaping into the Harlem Renaissance. Through the parties, the music, and a newfound friend, his life takes on new meaning. Dave's life begins to change.

Connection: Recklessness

Picture Book

📖 *The Wretched Stone* by Chris Van Allsburg. Boston: Houghton Mifflin, 1991.

Chris Van Allsburg has created an allegory about obsession. In excerpts from the log of the ship the *Rita Anne*, the captain relates the strange events of a voyage that begins with high hopes and ends in disaster. The first entries in the log describe a fine crew, not only accomplished in seamanship, but men who are readers, musicians, and storytellers. Indeed, the usual boredom of many days at sea is absent as the crew amuses each other with singing, dancing, and storytelling. One day the ship approaches an uncharted island, and the sailors go ashore to find fresh fruit. But none is to be found among the lush vegetation, nor are any animals or insects sighted. The crew do find a stone that glows, and the captain takes it aboard. The crew become fascinated with the stone and spend hours staring at it. Their gait slows and their posture stoops. When the captain states his intention of throwing the stone overboard, the crew lock themselves in the hold with the stone, leaving the captain to sail the ship alone, an impossible task. When the sailors emerge during a powerful storm, the captain is horrified to see they have become hairy beasts. He covers the stone and locks the compartment that holds it. The ship is too badly damaged to sail, and their only hope is to wait for rescue. Meanwhile, the captain reads to the crew and plays the violin. They begin walking upright and look more alert. "Those who knew how to read recovered more quickly." When rescue is at hand, the captain sets fire to the *Rita Anne*, sending the ship and the wretched stone to the bottom of the sea.

Discussion

1.   Can you identify the metaphor in this story? (Watching television.) Explain.

2.   What is the author saying about the value of music and literature?

3.   When can an obsession be good? When can it be dangerous?

Novel

📖 *The Crossing* by Gary Paulsen. Danbury, CT: Franklin Watts, 1987.

Sergeant Robert L. Locke's "wretched stone" is alcohol. He runs his life and his men by the book when on base but escapes across the Mexican border on weekends to drink his bad memories away. Manuel Bustos is an orphan trying to survive in a world where attack by gangs is always a threat. His obsession is to get to the United States. A strange love-hate relationship grows up between Manuel and the sergeant until the alcohol leaves Robert unable to defend himself from a gang attack. Manuel watches in hiding as his friend is killed, yet finds hope in the sergeant's billfold, which the gang missed. This is a gritty tale of how an obsession kills one man but gives the promise of a better life to a young boy.

Connection: Consequences of Carelessness

Picture Book

📖 *The Wreck of the Zephyr* by Chris Van Allsburg. Boston: Houghton Mifflin, 1983.

Why would there be a wreck of a small sailboat on top of cliffs high above the sea? An old man answers a visitor's question by telling of a boy who could sail a boat better than any other seaman. The boy often would set sail in bad weather to prove his skill. Bragging about his seamanship, the boy sets sail in a storm, is knocked out, and awakes to find his boat high upon the shore in a place where other boats sail high above the water. The people of the village offer to lead the boy to a safe path home, but he refuses to leave until he learns to fly his boat above the water. When, after several lessons, he is not able to do so, his teacher tells him it is time for him to go home. The boy takes his boat out late at night, determined to fly. For a time he succeeds, until he reaches his village. When he attempts to fly over the church tower so that all can see what a great sailor he is, his boat falls to the ground "with the sound of breaking branches and ripping sails." The boy escapes with a broken leg and never amounts to much. As the old sailor finishes his tale, he slowly limps away toward the harbor.

Discussion

1. How can exceptional talent lead to irresponsibility?

2. Cite instances from history in which talent has been misused.

3. Explain this statement: *Need alone is not enough to set power free.*

Novel

📖 *Johnny Tremain* by Esther Forbes. Boston: Houghton Mifflin, 1971.

Young Johnny Tremain, a young silversmith apprentice during the Revolutionary War, knows that he is the most talented of the apprentices. He is so confident of his skills that he breaks the rules. Working alone in the shop, he injures his hand so badly that his promising career as a master silversmith ends. Johnny, who pays dearly for his overconfidence, learns that there are many ways humans can contribute to society and find success in life.

Self-Identity

Connection: Finding One's Way

Picture Book

Goose by Molly Bang. New York: Blue Sky Press, 1999.

A violent storm blows a goose egg out of a nest, and it lands in the midst of a family of woodchucks. The woodchucks adopt the baby goose and teach it everything a youngster should know. But because she knows she is different from the others in her new family, the little goose is often sad. Nothing the woodchuck family does can cheer her up. The little goose leaves the family and sets out to see what she can discover. She finds no joy in the world around her and is so sad that she does not look where she is going and steps off a high cliff. She falls rapidly and seemingly to her death until she flaps her wings and discovers she can fly. She flies home, knowing now that she can cope with whatever life may bring.

Discussion

1. Do humans define themselves by who they are or what they do? Defend your answer.

2. How important is it to be surrounded by people who are like you?

3. Is running away the best way to solve a problem?

Novel

📖 *Nowhere to Call Home* by Cynthia deFelice. New York: Farrar, Straus & Giroux, 1999.

Twelve-year-old Frances lives comfortably with her father until the night he commits suicide. She is to be sent to live with an unfamiliar aunt in Chicago. Instead, she cashes in her ticket, buys some boys' clothes, cuts her hair, and embraces the life of a hobo. While riding the rails she meets Stewpot, a 15-year-old boy who pretends he does not know that Frances (Frankie) is a girl. He looks after her and protects her, teaching her the rules, routines, and language of the hobo world. Frances expected to find a life of freedom, but discovers one filled with squalor and acts of inhumanity. Stewpot's death finally makes her realize that the hobo life is not the answer to finding her place in the world.

Novel

📖 *Park's Quest* by Katherine Paterson. New York: E. P. Dutton, 1988.

Like the bold knights in his fantasies, young Park is on a quest. He wants to learn about his father, who died in Vietnam. However, he has no memory of his father, and his mother won't discuss him. When Park's search for family roots finally takes him to his grandfather's farm in rural Virginia, he encounters unimaginable obstacles. Instead of being welcomed as the long-lost heir, he is taunted by a sassy little foreigner, Thanh. Who is she, and what is she doing on the family farm? Worse, how dare she challenge him, Parkington Waddell Broughton V? Park must reconcile unsettling revelations about his parents, his uncle, his sick grandfather, and especially about Thanh before discovering the truth he has sought. In this warm, multilayered tale, an Arthurian legend is entwined with a contemporary odyssey.

Connection: Finding One's Identity

Picture Book

📖 *The Bunyip of Berkeley's Creek* by Jenny Wagner. Illustrated by Ron Brooks. New York: Puffin Books, 1974.

A strange thing happens in the black mud at the bottom of Berkeley's Creek. It happens in the middle of a dark night and frightens all the animals. It even frightens the strange thing himself, because he came from the mud of the creek, but he doesn't know who or what he is. It's a terrible thing not to have an identity. He asks everyone he meets, but no one can help identify him until the platypus comes along and reveals to him that he is a Bunyip. But what do Bunyips look like? Does he have feathers or fur? Does he have a nice tail? Is he handsome? No one gives him any positive answers and, most distressing of all, the scientist he meets says he doesn't exist at all! The Bunyip decides he must find his own identity. Things look grim and lonely until one dark night when another thing rises from the black mud and asks, "What am I?" The Bunyip knows the answer to that question and is delighted to tell her.

Discussion

1. What does it mean when we say, "It's not what's on the outside, but what's on the inside, that counts?"

2. George Bernard Shaw said that the worst sin toward our fellow creatures is not to hate them, but to be indifferent to them. Does this happen in school life? How?

3. What are some of the ways we can find our own identity? Who can help us in this search?

Novel

📖 *Even Stephen* by Johanna Hurwitz. Illustrated by Michael Dooling. New York: Morrow Junior Books, 1996.

Sunny knows how it is to grow up with a lot of problems. Her average grades, her need to wear glasses, and the failure to be noticed by the boys make her wish she were more like her popular brother, Stephen. He seems perfect in every way and she can't even get upset about it because he is always so good to her. Life goes on that way until tragedy strikes, and Stephen finds out that he is less than perfect. He fails when facing a life-and-death situation, and his failure almost destroys him. Stephen cannot face the fact that someone died. Now it is Sunny's chance to help her brother. She must find a way to show him that it was not his fault and that no one can do everything perfectly. Sunny finds the way and finds out why she is a valuable part of the family.

Novel

📖 *Hold Fast to Dreams* by Andrea Davis Pinkney. New York: Morrow Junior Books, 1995.

Moving to another town and starting at a new school is a very difficult thing for any 12-year-old girl. But if you're African-American and moving to an all-white world, that may be just the beginning of your problems. Deirdre knows this from her first bus trip to school. There will be many painful experiences while she learns to hold on to her dreams and her goals. Deirdre's sister, Lindsey, tries to "act white" and that does not work for her. However, Lindsey later finds her talent and happiness in sports. Deirdre's father successfully fights bigotry at work. Deirdre has her camera and her love for the poems of Langston Hughes. She uses both and finds her identity in dreams that come true.

Suicide

Connection: Coping with Suicide

Picture Book

📖 *I Never Knew Your Name* by Sherry Garland. Illustrated by Sheldon Greenberg. Boston: Houghton Mifflin, 1994.

A young boy who recently moved to a city apartment narrates this story as he observes a troubled neighbor boy. The older boy's tentative gestures of friendship are rejected by his peers. The boy tries to befriend a stray dog, and after watching others go off to the prom, cries as he feeds the pigeons on the roof. Several times the narrator thinks about trying to make friends with the boy but somehow never connects. At one point, the narrator and his sister make fun of the boy. The youngster ends his life by jumping from the rooftop. As the ambulance comes, the narrator regrets that he did not make a greater effort to befriend the boy. The strong message of the importance of reaching out to others is made clear without moralizing.

Discussion

1. Why are strangers often not welcome in a community?

2. If the narrator had tried to make friends with the boy, might the story have ended differently? Why or why not?

3. Why is it desirable to reach out to others who show a need for friendship?

Novel

📖 *Face at the Edge of the World* by Eve Bunting. New York: Clarion Books, 1988.

Charlie, a gifted young black writer, commits suicide. Jed, his best friend, is determined to retrace Charlie's last weeks in the town and the school, dubbed Suicide High, to discover the reason for such a senseless act. In his search for the truth, Jed discovers a secret girlfriend, a gang of dopers, and a private code. He begins to suspect that Charlie had been involved in illegal activities. A clue comes in a note given to Jed by Charlie's sister. He continues his quest and discovers the reason for the terrible anguish of Charlie's parents. As Jed pursues the truth, he interviews numerous people and discovers things not only about Charlie but also about himself. This suspenseful tale is not only about grief but also about love and friendship.

The Wages of War

Connection: Classic Struggles

Picture Book

📖 *The Illiad and the Odyssey*, retold and illustrated by Marcia Williams. Cambridge, MA: Candlewick Press, 1996.

Williams uses a comic book approach to depict Homer's telling of the ancient war between the Greeks and the Trojans and the involvement of the gods and goddesses of Mount Olympus in the lives of the mortals in ancient Greece. King Menelaus loses his beautiful wife, Helen, to Paris, who captures her heart and sails with her to Troy. Menelaus orders his greatest warrior, Odysseus, to take an army to destroy the Trojans and return with Helen. The battles are fierce, exciting, and seemingly unending. The use of the ruse of the Trojan horse brings victory, but the Greeks still face the horror of the Cyclops, the Lotus-Eaters, the Sirens, Circe, and Sylla on their sea voyage home. Only Athena can save Odysseus and return him to the surprise awaiting him at home.

Discussion

1. Why do you think people are interested in the ancient myths of Rome and Greece? How does the Trojan War compare to modern wars?

2. Troy was the setting for the classic story, *The Illiad.* What is the name of that ancient city today? How does the modern city compare with the city of the story?

3. Is this tale based on a true story? Has anyone ever found the remains of Homer's Troy?

Novel

📖 *Aleta and the Queen* by Priscilla Galloway. Toronto: Annick Press, 1995.

After the Trojan War, Odysseus and his warriors face a treacherous journey. Odysseus has offended one of the most powerful gods, Poseidon, who is the brother of Zeus. Only the help of another god or goddess can bring them through the terrors of the sea and the monsters that await them. Meanwhile, Odysseus's wife, Penelope, and his son, Telemachus, wait year after year for his return. The wait is dangerous because the leaders of Greece assume Odysseus is dead. Many of the leaders move into the palace and demand Penelope choose one of them to wed so there might be a new king and ruler. Penelope feels sure that Odysseus is alive and uses ploys to hold off the suitors. Aleta, the 12-year-old granddaughter of her servant, aids her. Aleta, wise and courageous, keeps many important secrets, playing a key role in the outcome of her queen's fate.

Novel

📖 *The Immortal* by Christopher Pike. New York: Pocket Books, 1993.

Josie is excited about her trip to Greece. She has learned about the history and the mystery of the ancient Greek people, their culture, and the islands that spread out through the Adriatic, Aegean, and Mediterranean

Seas. But she is not prepared for the twists and turns her life takes after she finds the statue of a goddess on one of the small islands. Josie joins the Immortals in their land beyond space and begins to realize the danger of being involved with them. They want something from her, something she is not willing to give—her life! Josie decides she must find a way to save herself. She returns to Mount Olympus, where, surprisingly, her camera comes to her aid. However, the sacrifice she makes to succeed sends her into another world.

Connection: Finding Courage

Picture Book

📖 *The Cello of Mr. O.* by Jane Cutler. Illustrated by Greg Couch. New York: E. P. Dutton, 1999.

In a city torn apart by war, Mr. O. lives in an upstairs apartment. He had once played his cello in the great concert halls, and people cheered and threw flowers. Now he is old and each Wednesday he lines up with the others in the building to get meager supplies from the truck that comes. On one particular Wednesday the line scatters as bombs fall, and the truck is destroyed. There will be no more supplies. On the following day Mr. O. brings a chair and his cello downstairs, sets it up in the town square, and begins to play. Somehow the music soothes the frightened people and Mr. O.'s courage spreads. The bombs return, and the cello is destroyed. But on the next day Mr. O. appears once again, takes a harmonica from his pocket, and begins to play, bringing hope to all who listen.

Discussion

1. Mr. O. brought courage to the people. In what other ways can individuals, no matter what their age, contribute to society?

2. What daily acts of courage might be found in the people of a city under siege?

3. List the many ways in which war can affect noncombatants.

Novel

📖 *The Eternal Spring of Mr. Ito* by Sheila Garrigue. New York: Bradbury Press, 1985.

Sent from London to live with relatives in Canada during World War II, young Sara becomes friends with the elderly Japanese gardener, Mr. Ito. He explains the meaning of the bonsai tree to Sara and shows her how to grow her own. Pearl Harbor is attacked and Sara's cousin's fiancé is killed. Her uncle is in charge of rounding up all Japanese and sending them to camps. Mr. Ito shows a special kind of courage, taking refuge in an isolated cave, going there to die. As hostility toward the Japanese increases, life with Sara's aunts becomes tense. Mr. Ito dies, and Sara promises to pass his bonsai tree on to his family. But how can she fulfill her promise when the camps are far away and anyone helping the Japanese is branded a traitor?

Novel

📖 *The Cay* by Theodore Taylor. New York: Doubleday, 1989.

Phillip's mother doesn't like black people. "They are not the same as you," she tells him. "They are different, and they live differently. That's the way it must be." Phillip had never believed her. After the Germans torpedo the freighter on which he and his mother are traveling from war-time Curacao to the United States, Phillip finds himself dependent on an old West Indian, who is black. Timothy is huge and very old. To Phillip, he seems ugly. He eats raw fish and is the most stubborn man Phillip has ever known. The two of them—three if you counted Stew Cat—are cast up on a barren little Caribbean island. A crack on the head and exposure to too much sun leave Phillip blind. Their struggle for survival and Phillip's efforts to adjust to his blindness and to understand the dignified, wise, and loving old man who is his companion make memorable reading.

Connection: Growing with Conflict

Picture Book

📖 *The Seed* by Isabel Pin. New York: North-South Books, 2001.

One day a seed drops from the sky and lands right on the border between two territories. The tribes on both sides immediately claim it. "This means war!" their leaders declare. "We must fight to win this seed for ourselves." Both sides prepare for battle with great inventiveness, creating huge arsenals of deadly weapons and drawing up complicated plans for attack. But ironically, in the midst of all these preparations, the seed itself quietly provides the simple solution the tribes had overlooked. The seed buries itself in the ground and grows into a cherry tree covered with blossoms, with branches long enough to reach out over both lands.

Discussion

1. Is ignoring conflict among nations a good way to deal with the devastation war brings?

2. Could this book symbolize the unawareness claimed by many Germans of the persecution of the Jews in that country? Why or why not?

3. In one minute, brainstorm words to describe war. In one more minute, brainstorm words to describe peace. Which list is longer? Why?

Novel

📖 *Lily's Crossing* by Patricia Reilly Giff. New York: Random House, 1997.

During World War II, Lily goes with her grandmother to Rockaway Beach to escape the heat of New York City. Lily is unhappy at the loss of her mother. Then her father leaves for the war front. When her best friend moves away, Lily can only find comfort in her fantasies. These fantasies lead to lies and danger when Lily befriends a war refugee, Albert, who comes from Hungary. Albert, desperate to return to Europe to find his sister, has also lost his parents and is overcome with guilt at having to leave his little sister behind in war-torn Europe. The two children share their lives and secrets and begin to understand the misery of war. Lily convinces Albert that he can swim into the ocean and catch one of the passing troop ships to get back to his sister. Albert almost loses his life trying. They both begin to grow in wisdom, and with the end of the war come events that seal their friendship forever.

Novel

Under the Blood-Red Sun by Graham Salisbury. New York: Bantam Doubleday, 1994.

War produces many victims, including innocent bystanders. World War II involved one of the most unfortunate and unfair instances of oppression of the innocent—of Japanese Americans when Pearl Harbor was bombed. Tomi suffers this oppression first-hand because his parents and grandparents were born in Japan. They live in Hawaii and are American citizens, but that doesn't seem to matter when the United States declares war on Japan. One day Tomi's life is happy and carefree, with no more to worry about than winning the next ball game. Then the planes with the blood-red symbol on them come screaming overhead, and his world turns red with death and destruction. Due to the fear and hatred, people lose their reason. Tomi's father and grandfather are put in prison. His mother loses her job, and former friends consider them the enemy. Tomi has only one thing to sustain him: his determination to protect the family sword and uphold the family pride. He needs help desperately and he receives it from an unexpected source.

Connection: Finding Hope

Picture Book

📖 *The Snow Goose* by Paul Gallico. New York: Random House, 1988.

Two people, crippled by their emotional and physical defects, find it difficult to express their love for each other. Philip Rayader is a hunchback, but he is also an artist. Frith, a young girl, knows poverty and loneliness. She feels empathy for a wounded snow goose and overcomes her initial fear of Philip to seek his help with the beautiful bird. It takes years of tentative and poignant attempts to understand each other before Philip and Frith begin to love each other. They work together to heal the bird and find great joy in following the progress of the snow bird, who chooses to make his home with Philip.

Life changes forever when the German army sweeps across Europe and drives thousands of English soldiers to the beaches of Dunkirk. They are trapped with the sea to their back and the Germans moving in for the kill. The only hope is with the fishermen and other Englishmen who could get into the shallow water with their small boats and take the men to the safety of the big transports waiting in the deep waters. Philip knows the danger, but he says good-bye to Frith, and with the snow goose flying overhead, he sails the English Channel to save others and to meet his destiny. Frith watches him depart, knowing he will not return. Later there comes a day when the snow goose returns for one last time, and Frith sees the return as a message of love and hope.

Discussion

1. Why do the greatest hardships in life bring out the strength and courage in some people and not in others?

2. Can evil bring about goodness? Why or why not?

3. What could cause a powerful leader to want to destroy a whole race of people?

4. Do we have an obligation to intercede when we see injustice?

Novel

📖 *Stones in the Water* by Donna Jo Napoli. New York: Dutton Children's Books, 1997.

Imagine sitting in a movie theater with your brother and several friends watching a great show when German soldiers suddenly burst in and capture all the men in the audience. Then imagine being transported to a slave camp miles and miles away from your family. This happens to Roberto, who lives in Venice, Italy, during World War II. On the terrifying trip to the camp, Roberto, separated from his brother, fears for his life. He also fears for his Jewish friend, Samuele. The trip to the slave camp is hellish, but what awaits the boys is even more nightmarish. They endure inhuman treatment, hunger, cold, and horror at witnessing what happens to the Jews in the camp. Life centers on survival. The boys try to help each other, which leads to a tragic end for Samuele. Roberto now realizes his only hope lies in escape, even though it means almost certain death. He finds his chance to flee, begins the struggle to stay alive against enormous odds, and faces decisions about the future if he ever reaches home.

Connection: The Aftermath of War

Picture Book

📖 *The Wall* by Eve Bunting. Illustrated by Ronald Himler. New York: Clarion Books, 1990.

There are many walls in the world: sea walls, decorative walls, and historic walls. But the saddest wall of all is the Wall commemorating victims of the Vietnam War that Dad and his young son visit in Washington, D.C. Dad goes there to find the name of his father and to share that experience with the boy. The Wall is black and shiny. It mirrors many sad faces as people try to find the names of their loved ones who died in Vietnam so far away from home. The boy sees a soldier without legs who stares at the wall from his wheelchair. He sees an old couple who cry when they find their son's name chiseled on the hard stone. He sees messages and pictures left lying against the wall and knows that they were left for those who can no longer collect them. To find grandpa's name, they have to find the right year. There are 58,000 names and the boy feels his father's sadness as they search for it. It is quiet as they make a rubbing of the name. The boy leaves his picture against the wall and tells Dad how proud he is of Grandpa, but that he'd rather have him here.

Discussion

1. Why was the Vietnam War so controversial?

2. What other American war was similar to Vietnam?

3. Why do you think the Wall is a good memorial to those who died in Vietnam?

Novel

📖 *December Stillness* by Mary Downing Hahn. New York: Clarion Books, 1988.

The horrors of war are responsible for changing people and their lives forever. Although peace comes, the aftermath of battle may last for a lifetime. Kelly is a high school student who is absorbed in her classes, her friends, and her looks. She knows little about the heroic sacrifices that were made in places like Vietnam by soldiers who were not much older than she is when they served. Kelly gets an insight into why there are troubled and homeless veterans when she meets Mr. Weems. People call him the bagman because he collects things from trash cans and carries them around in a big plastic bag. He spends the rest of his time in the public library reading books on Vietnam. Kelly interviews Mr. Weems for a research paper. Mr. Weems wants no part of the questioning or her attempts to help him. He dumps the sandwiches she makes for him in the trash and strikes out at those who try to keep him out of the library. Kelly finally finds a way to communicate with the homeless veteran, and his words give her a view into the Vietnam he calls hell. In spite of her help, Weems knows his only hope lies in another world. He becomes another casualty of the war and Kelly finds a way to include him on the Wall.

Novel

📖 *The Car* by Gary Paulsen. San Diego: Harcourt Brace, 1994.

Terry Anders is left with no parents and no family at the age of 14. Having nothing to lose, he decides to find an uncle he hardly knows and who lives in Oregon. The one thing he does have is a car, which his father left in pieces and which Terry put back together. Terry has an adventure traveling for a while by himself. But his experiences are richer after he meets Waylon Jackson, a Vietnam veteran. They hit it off from the start and travel the back roads of the country, where they face danger and narrow escapes. Terry has to grow up fast, and he learns how from Waylon. The veteran had a hard time in Vietnam and it left him with scars that Terry can barely understand. Terry only knows he would not want to cross Waylon. They visit Waylon's friends, and one of them joins in the journey through the Western states. It is dangerous because the two men find fights wherever they go. In the end, the police catch up with them, and Waylon convinces Terry to get away to safety. Terry drives for a few miles, but returns, realizing he can't leave the only family he knows.

Wisdom

Connection: Finding Wisdom

Picture Book

📖 *The Hunter: A Chinese Folktale* retold by Mary Casanova. Illustrated by Ed Young. New York: Scholastic, 2000.

Hai Li Bu lives in a Chinese village many years ago. As a hunter, he provides food for all the villagers. He loves his work, and the people love him for his generosity. There comes a year when a terrible drought visits the land, leading to much suffering and starvation. Hai Li Bu can do nothing to help until the day he saves the life of a small snake that turns out to be the enchanted daughter of the Dragon King of the sea. As a reward, the king gives Hai Li Bu the ability to understand the language of the animals. Now he can find food for his people. The king cautions him to tell no one of the reward or he will be turned to stone. Hai Li Bu saves the village by listening to the animals, but when he also learns about the great flood that will soon come, the people will not believe him. They cannot understand how he knows such things, and they refuse to flee the village. In desperation, Hai Li Bu tells them the secret and turns to stone. Only then do the villagers realize they should have had faith in his words. They make a shrine of the stone and resolve from then on to listen to good advice, from the village's eldest to the youngest.

Discussion

1. What is your definition of *wisdom*?

2. Can wisdom be found in young people? Give an example.

3. Does wisdom always increase with age?

Novel

Yossi Tries to Help God by Miriam Chaikin. Illustrated by Denise Saldutti. New York: Harper & Row, 1987.

Yossi, a Jewish boy, lives in Brooklyn. He is very involved with family, school, and religion. He is particularly interested in being charitable toward others and is motivated by the stories his teacher tells of Aaron-the-peacemaker, who went around doing good deeds and patching up quarrels between friends. When Yossi's little sister becomes very sick he tries to find a way to help, but all he can think of is something his teacher told him about making an angel when you do a good deed. Yossi decides he must make one to help his sister get well. The good deed he chooses is to make peace between two boys who had become enemies. All of his efforts only make things worse between the two boys, and Yossi is desperate to make things right to get an angel for his sister. He turns to his teacher for direction and finds that his good deed must be a wise one and it must come from the heart. He realizes that he has been more intent on making an angel than doing a good deed. However, between the two of them they find a way to create the angel they need.

Novel

📖 *Switchers* by Kate Thompson. New York: Hyperion, 1998.

Tess, who lives in Ireland with her family, has a secret that she can share with no one, not even her mother or father. She knows that no one would believe that a girl could become any animal she decides on—that she is a switcher. Tess escapes her life whenever she chooses by turning herself into a squirrel, a rabbit, a wolfhound, or a terrier. But although she finds freedom and adventure with no fear for her safety, she is always alone to protect that secret. As the years pass, she learns how to change with more adeptness. All goes well until a boy, who seems to know too much, follows Tess. Kevin reveals himself as another switcher who needs Tess's help for a quest he has undertaken. The animal world has enlisted his help to save the Northern Hemisphere from destruction by a deadly iciness. Kevin cannot do it alone, and Tess reluctantly joins the struggle. The two of them assume one animal form after another in their battle against evil. Their common purpose turns them into friends. They face danger together, but which one will make the ultimate sacrifice?

Witchcraft

Connection: Facing Witchcraft

Picture Book

📖 *The Red Heels* by Robert San Souci. New York: Dial Books, 1995.

Jonathan Dowse, an itinerant shoemaker, travels the roads of colonial New England. Lost in the woods, he comes upon a small cabin inhabited by a beautiful young girl, Rebecca Wyse. He enters a room dancing with shadows and warmed by the glow of the fireplace. Rebecca shows him a pair of worn-out shoes with red heels that belonged to her mother and grandmother and asks him to make her new shoes to fit the heels. Jonathan is reluctant to do so, knowing that the country folk believe that red heels are a sign of witchcraft. Rebecca has such a gentle manner that he gives in and makes the shoes. That night he watches in secret as Rebecca dons the shoes and flies up the chimney. Unable to resist, and haven fallen in love with the girl, he follows her and dances with her in the moonlight high above the forest. As the sun rises, Jonathan knows that he must return to the real world and Rebecca must choose between Jonathan and giving up her "secret delight." Readers will relate to this romantic tale that can serve as a springboard to more realistic fiction about witchcraft.

Discussion

1. Was Rebecca truly a witch, or was Jonathan bewitched by love?

2. In what way could this tale be a metaphor for choices inherent in women's liberation?

Novel

📖 *Gallows Hill* by Lois Duncan. New York: Delacorte Press, 1997.

Sarah's mother takes her from her familiar surroundings in California to a new home in Missouri. Mom, in love with the local married, tyrannical schoolteacher, becomes the "other woman." Sarah is unhappy with the move but agrees to play a fortuneteller at a school event. She does it so well that one of the most popular boys convinces her to take up fortune telling as a business. She is too successful; the fortunes begin coming true. Sarah's dreams of the Salem Witch trials turn to reality when she and several other students are found to be reliving the past lives of those who were put to death in Salem.

Novel

📖 *The Witch of Blackbird Pond* by Elizabeth George Speare. New York: Laurel Leaf Books, 1978.

In 1687, Kit Tyler is an adventurous young woman who has lived all her life on the island of Barbados, where she was able to grow up with few restrictions. But after her grandfather dies she is sent to live with her mother's sister in the North American colonies. She boards a trading ship bound for Connecticut and instantly feels at home among the sailors. When the ship arrives, Kit is so excited that she cannot wait for the ship to make it to shore. She jumps on board one of the small boats and she and several other passengers paddle to shore. One small girl drops her doll over the side of the boat, and Kit jumps into the water to rescue the doll. When she reaches the boat she finds that her rash action has created displeasure among those watching. Kit's new life is filled with doing chores and attending Meeting, the long Puritan service. Her severely restricted life is made more bearable when the Widow Tupper, who is also suspected by the townspeople of being a witch, befriends her. Kit has much to learn and many challenges to face if she is ever to find happiness in this strange new world.

Working Together

Connection: Collaborating

Picture Book

📖 *The Eagle and the Wren, a Fable* retold by Jane Godall. Illustrated by Alexander Reichstein. New York: North-South Books, 2000.

This classic fable tells of a long-ago time when all the birds of the land boast about which one can fly the highest, sing the most beautifully, see the farthest, and the like. The owl suggests a contest to determine who can fly the highest. All the birds take to the air. After flying for quite a while, some of them grow tired and can fly no higher. The mighty eagle, extremely proud and sure of victory, soars so high he seems to reach the heavens. An unexpected occurrence shows him the meaning of humility, how valuable everyone's talents are, and what can be accomplished when those talents are combined.

Discussion

1. Does each of us have some special talent that can be used to accomplish something?

2. Do you believe that if we combined these talents there would be greater results? Give some examples.

3. What event in history can you think of when people accomplished a great feat by working together?

Novel

Willie the Frog Prince by C. S. Adler. New York: Clarion Books, 1994.

Willie is 11 years old, and every year has been filled with problems for him. Willie never seems to do anything right. His father never misses a chance to remind him of that fact. Willie can't concentrate on his math, and his spelling isn't much better. He thinks he could learn better with no distractions, but even sitting under the teacher's desk doesn't help his schoolwork. On top of all his other problems, Willie's dad has lost his job and has a lot of time to check up on Willie's lack of progress. His father also has time to fight with Willie's mother about the situation, which makes Willie feel very guilty. Willie meets Marla and things begin to look up. He feels a special bond with Marla because she has more problems than he has. Willie is determined to help her if he can. Willie knows how much Marla needs him and finds the right words to convince her of what she must do to save her family.

Novel

What's to Be Scared of, Suki? by C. S. Adler. New York: Clarion Books, 1996.

Suki has the usual problems of 13-year-old girls, but she also is very frightened of dogs. That is a serious problem for her because Justin, the boy she's interested in, has a big German shepherd. Her best friend, Allison, tries to help Suki overcome her fears, but they are too deep seated. Suki is caught up in her own problems until she realizes that

Justin's worries are much more important than her own. She decides to solve her problems first and has her chance when an overnight campout is planned with the German shepherd as part of it. Suki wonders if she will die of fright before the campout. However, her problems seem unimportant when Justin faces life-threatening abuse at his father's hands. Suki shares her love and understanding with Justin, and in return he helps her overcome her fear. Together, they create a happy ending.

Part 2

LURES TO LANGUAGE

Alliteration

Picture Books

📖 *Some Smug Slug* by Pamela Duncan Edwards. New York: HarperCollins, 1996.

A slug slowly slithers up a steep slope, ignoring the warnings of sparrow, spider, swallowtail, a snickering skunk, and a scolding squirrel. In the end, the slug discovers that the sly, slippery slope was a sham. This is a silly, suspenseful saga with a surprise ending that makes its point through alliteration.

📖 *Fed Up! A Feast of Frazzled Foods* by Rex Barron. New York: Putnam, 2000.

Have you ever met an Anxious Apple, Impatient Ice Cream, or a Zucchini practicing Zen? Whether they are about to be eaten, melting in the hot sun, or relaxing in a Japanese garden, Rex Barron's eye-catching characters, with many of them on the verge of being eaten, are altogether hilarious, dramatic, and so nearly human. Did you know, for example, that Fig fights Fat, Garlic gobbles Germs, and Lemons loathe Limes? In this fresh ABC book for all ages you will encounter irresistible fruits, vegetables, and other favorite foods that bring new meaning to the food chain and a dose of humor to eating.

📖 *The Z Was Zapped* by Chris Van Allsburg. Boston: Houghton Mifflin, 1987.

An alliterative alphabet book in which the "A was in an avalanche" and the "B was badly bitten." The illustrations offer many other alliterative possibilities.

Writing Prompt

Fill in the blanks with words starting with the same letter that will help you describe a person, place, or animal. Example:

A turtle's favorite letter is C

because

it is *cautious*,

contented,

and *capable*.

Its name is *Clem*.

It lives in *Cleveland*.

It *carefully* eats *carrots* and *cabbage*.

Anagrams

Picture Book

📖 *Elvis Lives and Other Anagrams* by Jon Agee. Boston: Farrar, Straus & Giroux, 2000.

Albert Einstein probably knew that by rearranging the letters in his name he could form the words "ten elite brains." He also might have known that an anagram is a word or phrase formed by transposing or jumbling the letters in another word or phrase. Here, in Jon Agee's book of word play, hilarious illustrations are paired with more than 16 of the greatest anagrams in the English language. But watch out, once you get started you will be rearranging the letters in your name, your mother's name, or the name of your teacher, your town, or your pet iguana.

Writing Prompt

Rearrange the letters in the following phrases to identify movies, television shows, and actors. Example: Total fanatic rat = Fatal Attraction

MOVIES

1. Oddest killers
2. My, a monster
3. Three mental cripples
4. His itchy ego
5. Stale article
6. Three chasers
7. Warn weirdo
8. A born worker
9. Rank Romeo
10. Huge ring theft

TELEVISION SHOWS

1. My dismal fathead
2. Motivate unfair army
3. Finally the maid
4. Had spy pay
5. OK, up trash
6. Shh, cowboy set
7. Gosh, weirdo mode

ACTORS

1. Cool energy ego
2. Rich red socks
3. Friendly jeers
4. No aliens, darling
5. Satire likely

Anagrams reprinted with permission of Traviss Willcox from the Web site http://www.anagrams.net.

Answers

MOVIES

1. Oddest killers = Dressed to Kill
2. My, a monster = Smart Money
3. Three mental cripples = The Scarlet Pimpernel
4. His itchy ego = High Society
5. Stale article = Little Caesar
6. Three chasers = The Searchers
7. Warn weirdo = Rear Window
8. A born worker = Broken Arrow
9. Rank Romeo = Moonraker
10. Huge ring theft = The Gunfighter

TELEVISION SHOWS

1. My dismal fathead = The Addams Family
2. Motivate unfair army = My Favorite Martian
3. Finally the maid = All in the Family
4. Had spy pay = Happy Days
5. OK, up trash = South Park
6. Shh, cowboy set = The Cosby Show
7. Gosh, weirdo mode = Doogie Howser, M.D.

ACTORS

1. Cool energy ego = George Clooney
2. Rich red socks = Rick Schroder
3. Friendly jeers = Jerry Seinfeld
4. No aliens, darling = Gillian Anderson
5. Satire likely = Kirstie Alley

Biography Poems

Picture Book

📖 *The Microscope* by Maxine Kumin. New York: HarperCollins, 1984.

"They called him dumbkopf, that means dope. That's how we got the microscope." These are the closing words of a lilting biography of the Dutch shopkeeper, Anton Leeuwenhoek, whose fascination with glass lenses led him to ignore the demands of everyday life. Told in verse, the story tells us that he neglected his shop while discovering things not visible to the human eye; creatures swimming in a drop of blood and bugs in the water that we drink. His obsession resulted in his becoming known as the Father of Microbiology.

Writing Prompt

After researching the life of a person you choose, use Maxine Kumin's model to explain the major characteristics that led the person to fame. Example:

MARY HARRIS JONES

Mary Harris Jones was old
At ninety-three she still was bold as brass!
She'd hop right on the nearest train
Put on her hat and go raise Cain.
She had no home, no money, no kin
But was interested in
The workers' plight.
She traveled east and south and west,
Exhorting men to do their best
To hold out in their strikers' lines
Against the owners of the mines.
Of the hardships that she tells
Were cold and hunger, cat call yells,
And worst of all the constant fear
That she might lose.
"Take her away," the owners said.
"Prison's what she needs instead."
This woman's never-ending fight
Against the workers' awful plight
Brought her close to death at times
From owners' guns at strikers' lines.
Hated by one, revered by the other
Stuck to her cause and acclaimed as
Mother Jones

Descriptive Writing

Picture Book

📖 *Toad* by Ruth Brown. New York: E. P. Dutton, 1997.

No matter how many words one can come up with to describe a toad, Ruth Brown has even more. Using rhyming text and detailed water color illustrations, the author/artist creates a truly memorable creature. Toad is "odorous, oozing, foul and filthy and he leaves a slimy trail." He is covered with warts and lumps and bumps, and because he is not a very graceful fellow he stumbles along his way straight into the jaws of a monster. Because toad is so noxious, the monster spits him out (in a colorful two-page spread) and toad goes along his way as happy and contented as before. Here is an outstanding example of close observation followed by descriptive writing.

Writing Prompt

Choose a political cartoon from the newspaper. Write a paragraph describing the cartoon for someone who has never seen it. Use as many descriptive words as possible.

Exaggeration

Picture Books

📖 *Sally Ann Thunder Ann Whirlwind Crockett* by Steven Kellogg. New York: Morrow Junior Books, 1995.

Who is the toughest living creature on the entire old frontier? Why, none other than Sally Ann Thunder Ann Whirlwind. On the day she was born she could out-talk, out-grin, out-scream, out-swim, and out-run any baby in Kentucky, and in a few years she was more than a match for bears, rattlers, alligators, and even the mighty Mike Fink. But when Sally Ann rescued Davy Crockett from a pair of rampaging eagles, even her hornet's nest bonnet and skunk perfume didn't stop him from proposing marriage.

📖 *Swamp Angel* by Anne Isaacs. Illustrated by Paul O. Zelinsky. New York: E. P. Dutton, 1994.

When Angelica Longrider is born, she is scarcely taller than her mother and can't climb a tree without help. She is a full two years old before she builds her first log cabin. By the time she is fully grown, Swamp Angel can lasso a tornado and drink an entire lake dry. She single-handedly saves the settlers from the fearsome bear known as Thundering Tarnation, wrestling him from the top of the Great Smoky Mountains to the bottom of a deep lake. That night Tarnation feeds everyone in Tennessee and "you could hear the waistcoat buttons popping as far away as Kentucky."

Writing Prompt

Write several sentences using exaggeration to describe an extremely hot or very cold day. Example: Folks said it was hot enough to fry an egg on the sidewalk. Nobody could prove that fact, though. It was so hot that all the eggs the hens laid were hardboiled.

Metaphor/Personification

Picture Book

📖 *Grandfather Twilight* by Barbara Berger. New York: Philomel Books, 1984.

This seemingly simple picture book is an extraordinary example of metaphor and personification. Day is done, shadows begin to deepen, and it is time for Grandfather Twilight to go for his walk through the forest to welcome the night. As he walks he carries a small pearl that grows and begins to glow as he reaches the sea. "Gently he gives the pearl to the silence of the sea." Grandfather Twilight makes his way home, pats his faithful dog, climbs into bed, and goes to sleep.

Writing Prompt

Create a paragraph about daybreak, night, or morning using metaphors and personification. Example:

I am Grandmother Twilight putting the sun to bed behind towering mountain tops. In my hand I hold a lighted match that flickers and then dies, leaving my cousin, Night, to celebrate the dawn.

Picture Book

📖 *Grandmother Winter* by Phyllis Root. Illustrated by Beth Krommes. Boston: Houghton Mifflin, 1999.

All through the spring, summer, and fall, Grandmother Winter tends her geese and gathers their feathers to stuff in her quilt. Why? To bring snowfall as she shakes the quilt, snowfall as soft as feathers and bright as a winter moon. Krommes provides an excellent example of the use of metaphor to describe a natural phenomenon.

Writing Prompt

What metaphors can be used to describe a desert, a mountain, or an ocean?

A. List things the ocean reminds you of.
    Example: a watery curtain (metaphor)

B. List things the ocean does that a person does.
    Example: Trembles (personification)

C. List how, where, or when it does B.
    Example: When a storm takes the stage

D. Choose from each list and put together one line using personification and metaphor.
    Example: The ocean is a watery curtain that trembles when a storm takes the stage.

Picture Book

📖 *Workshop* by Andrew Clements. Illustrated by David Wisnieski. New York: Clarion Books, 1999.

This book contains fine examples of personification as each tool in a workshop takes on human qualities. A young apprentice watches and helps many craftsmen work to create a turn-of-the-century carousel. In the hands of these masters, drills are patient, saws bite, knives are edgy, the toolbox remembers, and the "ax finds the board that hides the log." In the end the craftsmen give a gift of tools to the apprentice as they admire the finished carousel.

Writing Prompt

Choose something familiar to personify. Example: Desk is a hugger. Desk turns thinkers into writers. Write a poem personifying that thing. Example:

The Chalkboard

By the end
of the
day
the chalkboard
behind the teacher's
desk
wears the caked-on
swirls
and smears
of many
erasings:
the strange
make-up
of
my teacher's
Teaching.

Keith Polette

News Article

Picture Book

📖 *The Egyptian News* by Scott Steedman. Cambridge, MA: Candlewick Press, 1996.

The author presents information using a newspaper format and including various sections of a typical newspaper from breaking news stories (King Tut Murdered?) to want ads and social events. Major news stories use the basic news format, with essential information given in the first paragraph and details of lesser and lesser importance in the paragraphs that follow.

Writing Prompt

Study the major news stories presented in *The Egyptian News* as well as the example that follows. Using one major event from a favorite novel, rewrite it as a basic news story.

June 12, 1870
Hannibal, Missouri

LOCAL BOYS FEARED DROWNED

Funeral services will be held Thursday at 10:00 a.m. at Christ Church for Thomas Sawyer, Joseph Harper and Huckleberry Finn, all of Hannibal, who are presumed drowned. The boys have not been seen or heard from since June 6th when it was reported by Sawyer's cousin, Sid Sawyer, that he saw Tom, Joe Harper and Huck Finn all heading toward the river where "they were going to do some fishing."

A search organized by Sheriff Dobbs has been unproductive in discovering the missing boys. According to Dobbs, "We spent the last two days dynamiting the river, but all we turned up was a bundle of carp and six catfish. I figure the undertow got those boys. Who knows where they'll turn up?"

When reached for comment, Mrs. Polly Sawyer, Tom's aunt, said, "It's simply tragic, tragic I tell you. I don't know how I can endure this horrible turn of events. Oh, my poor, poor Tom."

Nonfiction Narrative

Picture Book

White Bear, Ice Bear by Joanne Ryder. New York: Morrow Junior Books, 1989.

White Bear, Ice Bear is one volume in an innovative series of picture books by the award-winning children's author Joanne Ryder about animals and their lives. Each Just for a Day book invites readers to enter the natural world in an imaginative way by becoming an animal in its environment for a day. Each is a blend of factual information and haunting literary style. Begin your adventure: become a polar bear. Imagine being large and powerful and wild, living at the top of the world. You are warm and safe, covered with thick fur, as winds blow around you. Imagine roaming over ice-covered seas, resting, hunting, and exploring icy cliffs in the dark Arctic winter. For a few hours, this faraway world is your home. Come be a polar bear, just for a day.

Writing Prompt

Using Joanne Ryder's format, tell about a historical incident as if you were an eyewitness. Example:

A DAY IN CHURCH: 1775

One Sunday morning you awaken to rays of sunshine streaming in your window. Church bells call in the distance, "Come out, come out."

You dress quickly, race down the stairs and open the door. Outside everything is different. You look down at your clothing. You, too, are different. You are a child of 1775.

Your homespun shirt and white stockings feel scratchy. Your copper buckled shoes pinch your feet and you climb aboard the wagon that will take you to church.

There are mutterings all around as you walk into church with your family. You hear the words "Dirty Tory" aimed at your father. You see heads turn away. Then you catch your breath as you look at the speaker in the pulpit: Thomas Paine. You hear his words. "We may as well assert that because a child has thrived on milk, that it was never meant to have meat or that the first twenty years of our lives is to become a precedent for the next twenty."

"But England is our parent country," your father shouts.

"Then more shame upon her conduct." Paine replies. "Even brutes do not devour their young nor savages make war upon their families."

The crowd mumbles and surges toward your father. He grasps you firmly and with head high, marches out of the church and then stops short as he reaches the wagon. Your horse is gone, taken, you know, by those who are no longer loyal to the king.

A loud hymn coming from the church surrounds you, lifts you, and carries you back to the door of your home. You open the door and step inside. The world of 1775 fades and you are once again a child of the twenty-first century.

Opposites

Picture Book

📖 *Fortunately* by Remy Charlip. New York: Four Winds Press, 1964.

In a series of opposite actions, the author tells about a boy who has a hard time getting to a party because of the unfortunate things that happen. When the boy takes a plane, the motor explodes. He has a parachute, but it has a hole in it. There is a haystack to land in, but it has a pitchfork in it. Fortunately, an opposite event makes things turn out right.

Writing Prompt

Use Charlip's model to write a story using a series of opposite events. Example:

Fishing Expedition by Keith Polette

Good News:	I was fishing in a small boat off the coast of Florida late one calm, summer evening.
Bad News:	The boat sprung a hole and began to sink.
Good News:	I had a life preserver in the boat.
Bad News:	But by the time I turned to reach for it, the life preserver had floated away.
Good News:	I knew how to swim.
Bad News:	The shore was three miles away and I was too tired to make it there.
Good News:	I found something in the water to hang on to.
Bad News:	Suddenly, though, it moved.
Good News:	It was a dolphin.
Bad News:	I held on, but the dolphin began swimming too fast, and I kept gulping water, causing me to cough.
Good News:	I looked up and saw that we were close to shore.

Bad News:	The dolphin dumped me and took off in the opposite direction.
Good News:	As I sank I hit bottom and found that I was in four feet of water.
Bad News:	As my feet hit the sand, a jellyfish stung me.
Good News:	I was able to hobble to shore.
Bad News:	When I got to shore I couldn't walk any farther.
Good News:	I found a blanket to sit on; then I fell asleep.
Bad News:	I began dreaming that I was fishing in a small boat off the coast of Florida one calm summer night.

Palindromes

Picture Book

So Many Dynamos by Jon Agee. New York: Farrar, Straus & Giroux, 1993.

These palindromes will challenge the most able writer. Each phrase reads the same backward or forward. The droll black-and-white cartoon illustrations add to the fun of the book. For example, two nuns are sitting at a bar and one says to the other, "Flo, gin is a sin, I golf." By separating the letters the same phrase can be read backwards. The author/artist offers more palindromes in his follow-up book, *Sit on a Potato Pan, Otis!*

Writing Prompt

Research lists of palindromes and try your hand at writing a phrase that can be read the same backward or forward. Example: The title of Jon Agee's newest book on palindromes is *Go Hang a Salami! I'm a Lasagna Hog!* (New York: Farrar, Straus & Giroux, 1994).

Parody: Cinderella

Picture Books

📖 *Ashpet: An Appalachian Tale* by Joanne Compton. Illustrated by Kenn Compton. New York: Holiday House, 1996.

Long ago, in a cabin by Eagle's Nest Mountain, lives a serving girl called Ashpet. All day long she washes clothes, chops firewood, cooks, and cleans for the Widow Hooper and her cranky daughters. Ashpet has so much work to do, the widow won't even allow her to go to the annual church picnic. Ashpet's life changes for the better, however, when old Granny shows up and works some magic. She manages to outshine the widow's daughters and win the heart of the doctor's son.

📖 *Bigfoot Cinderrrrrella* by Tony Johnston. Illustrated by James Warhola. New York: Putnam, 1998.

Both Cinderella and her prince are big, furry, and smelly and live in an old growth forest world where these are signs of great beauty. Bigfoot Prince plans to select one of the smelly maidens as his bride at the annual funfest. She must not only be big, hairy, and smelly but also must be a nature lover like the prince. Rrrrrella, who has feet like log canoes, will be a perfect match, and it is a grizzly bear who serves as her "beary godfather" to help her get to the funfest in time.

📖 *Bubba the Cowboy Prince: A Fractured Texas Tale* by Helen Ketteman. Illustrated by James Warhola. New York: New York: Scholastic, 1997.

Bubba, the stepson of a wicked cattle rancher, is reviled and over-worked by his brothers, Dwayne and Milton. He wants to go to Miz Lureen's ball, along with countless other suitors. Miz Lureen is a wealthy neighbor who wants a man to help her work her spread. She wouldn't mind if he was attractive as well. With the help of a fairy godcow, Bubba goes to the ball and loses his boot. Miz Lureen manages to find Bubba and they ride off together to a life of happy ranching.

📖 *Cinder Edna* by Ellen Jackson. Illustrated by Kevin O'Malley. Lothrop, 1994.

Downtrodden, passive Cinderella lives next door to activist Cinder Edna, who is also poor. Whereas Cinderella does nothing but take the abuse of her stepmother and stepsisters, Cinder Edna does not depend on a fairy godmother to make her life better. She earns money by doing jobs such as mowing lawns and cleaning parrot cages. When she gets to the ball (by bus, of course) she finds the prince is a less-than-eligible bache-lor. In fact, he is so boring that Cinder Edna finds Rupert, the prince's brother, far more entertaining. He can dance, tell jokes, and even discuss serious subjects like ecology. The end of the tale contrasts Cinderella and her prince, bored with the public events they must attend, with Cin-der Edna and Rupert, living happily ever after in their solar-heated cottage.

📖 *Cinder-Elly* by Frances Minters. Illustrated by G. Brian Karas. New York: Viking, 1994.

The setting is New York City and Cinder-Elly is unable to go to a basketball game for lack of a cool outfit. Fairy Godmother arrives as a somewhat overweight lady with a cane and shopping cart. Not only does she give Cinder-Elly the latest in outfits, she changes a garbage can into a bike so that she can get to the game. Her curfew is ten o'clock rather than midnight, and she loses a glass sneaker. The tale is told in rhyme.

📖 *Cinderella Skeleton* by Robert San Souci. Illustrated by David Catrow. Harcourt, 2000.

At first glance Boneyard Acres might seem like any run down, decayed graveyard, but if you look more closely, you'll meet Cinderella Skeleton, as sweetly foul as she can be. You might think that Cinderella Skeleton is the happiest ghoul in the land, but her two evil stepsisters treat her with scorn and leave her with all the housework and more. Enter Prince Charnel, the heartthrob of Halloween. As sure as bats fly and witches moan, Cinderella Skeleton steals his heart.

📖 *Cinderella's Rat* by Susan Meddaugh. Boston: Houghton Mifflin, 1997.

While attempting to escape with his sister, Ruth, from a trap, a rat is suddenly transformed into a coach boy. Then an imposing old woman orders him to drive a beautiful young girl to the palace. There he and his sister (who is still a rat) discover a fully stocked pantry. When another castle boy sees Ruth he shouts, " A rat! Kill it." When the coach boy rat manages to save Ruth from death, he decides the services of a wizard are needed to change Ruth into a girl. The inept wizard first changes Ruth into a cat, then a girl who meows, then a girl who barks. Before the wizard can undo his last spell, the clock strikes midnight and the coach boy once again becomes a rat. Ruth helps her family by keeping the cats away.

📖 *Cinderhazel: The Cinderella of Halloween* by Deborah Lattimore. New York: Scholastic, 1997.

Cinderhazel loves attacking dirt with her broom. "That's what I'm good at," she says. While the cruel stepsisters prepare for the Witches Halloween Ball, Cinderhazel can only be tempted to go to Prince Alarming's palace by being told it has 15 filthy fireplaces. Since Prince Alarming likes to attack dirt as much as Cinderhazel, they finally get together and live "filthily ever after."

📖 *Dinorella* by Pamela Duncan Edwards. Illustrated by Henry Cole. New York: Hyperion, 1997.

Dinorella lives in the dunes and is treated dreadfully by her stepsisters, Dora and Doris. Naturally she is not allowed to go to Duke Dudley's dance, but with the help of Fairydactyl she manages to save

Duke Dudley from being devoured by a dastardly dionitchus. Using al-literation, the author retells the traditional Cinderella tale by setting it in the stone age and making the heroine a dinosaur. The number of "D" words she uses is truly dazzling!

Writing Prompt

Write a Cinderella parody. Before writing, answer the following questions:

- In your tale, what is her name?
- Where would she live?
- What jobs would she have to do?
- What foods would she have to prepare?
- Who would the stepsisters want to marry?
- How would the stepsisters be dressed?
- What transportation is used in this time and place?
- What would be the event everyone would want to attend?
- Who would help Cinderella? How?
- What would her dress look like?
- What would she lose? How?

Using the following example, decide on a setting (graveyard, outer space, health club, etc.) and a time (past, present, future) for your Cinderella parody. Be sure that every word you insert in place of the numbers in the story reflects the time and place you are writing about. For some tales, research may be necessary.

Title: _____

In a (1) just around the corner from (2) there lived a young girl named (3). Twenty-four hours a day she worked in the (4) a virtual slave to her wicked stepmother (5) and her two greedy and selfish stepsisters (6) and (7). "Oh, dear," she cried, "I shall never, ever finish all this work that Stepmother had given me to do. I have to (8) and then prepare the (name foods 9) for her to take to the (10)."

"What is that I hear?" asked one ugly sister. It must be (11) approaching in a (12). Quick, let's adorn ourselves in (13) and go to greet (14)." "Look how handsome he is, all dressed up in (15).

The stepmother and her daughters took the food and climbed into/on the (16). Off they went to enjoy the (17), leaving (18) all alone, surrounded by a mountain of (19). Suddenly there was a (20) at the door. It was (21) who took one look at the mess and waved his/her/its (22). In a (23) the work was all done and a beautiful (clothing 24) and (footwear 25) appeared. This beautiful adornment, however, would become rags once again when (26) so (27) must be home by then.

At the (28) the (29) (male character) asked (30) to (31). The time went so quickly that she realized she must leave at once. She reached for her (32) and threw it (33) and ran home.

(34) (male character) was distraught. He traveled year after year throughout the (35) searching for the maiden that the (36) would fit. Many years passed. The (37) (male character), who was now gray and wrinkled, faced many dangers in his travels such as (38). But he never gave up his quest.

Then one day he chanced to come upon the (39) (dwelling) of the stepmother and stepsisters who were now as old and wrinkled as he. "Try on the (40) that old man is holding? I should say not," the stepsisters screamed. "Let (41) try it on. She is getting so old she can't work the way she used to. Get out here, (42)!"

Before (43) could try on the (44) she gazed into (45) eyes.

Complete the tale by telling how the male character recognizes the girl, spirits her away, and leaves a just punishment for the stepmother and stepsisters.

Parody: Fairy Tales

Picture Books

📖 *The Frog Prince Continued* by Jon Scieszka. Illustrated by Steve Johnson. New York: Puffin Books, 1994.

The Frog Prince and his princess don't get along, so he seeks the help of witches from other fairy tales to turn him back into a frog again. In the end he decides life with the princess wasn't so bad after all and returns to her. When they kiss, both of them turn into frogs.

📖 *Hansel and Pretzel* by Mike Thaler. Illustrated by Jared Lee. New York: Scholastic, 1997.

Ignoring their parents' warning not to go in the woods, Hansel and Pretzel find themselves lost. They come upon a gingerbread house and while they argue whether or not it belongs to a witch, the door opens and a witch with a green pickle nose invites them to dinner. After the witch puts Hansel in a cage to fatten him up, Pretzel tells him to "Look on the bright side. At least we're not lost anymore." When Hansel escapes from the cage and the witch chases him, she accuses him of being "fast food." In the end, the children escape and the witch "stopped being hard-boiled and became a vegetarian."

📖 *Jim and the Beanstalk* by Raymond Briggs. New York: Coward, 1989.

In this modern version of the traditional tale, Jim is an adventurous boy who sees a plant growing past his high rise apartment window. He climbs the plant and discovers a very old giant who has no teeth or hair and can't see to read his poetry books. When Jim suggests glasses, the giant shows him his beer glasses. Jim explains about reading glasses, measures the giant's head, and with money the giant gives him, has special glasses made. Next come the giant-sized false teeth and a bright red wig. Jim and the giant part friends, but Jim decides that future visits would be unwise because the giant can once again eat "fried boys on toast."

📖 *Help Yourself, Little Red Hen!* by Alvin Granowsky. Illustrated by Wendy Edelson. Chatham, NJ: Raintree Steck-Vaughn, 1996.

This is one of a series of tales from a different point of view, in which the little red hen is so dependent on others that she can do nothing for herself. Her friends decide to teach her a lesson and each refuses to give help when asked. "You can do it," they tell her. In the end she finds that she can accomplish tasks without help; then she refuses to share her bread with others.

📖 *Rumpelstiltskin's Daughter* by Diane Stanley. New York: Morrow Junior Books, 1997.

Who would want to marry a king who will put a young girl to death if she does not spin straw into gold? Not Meredith. She marries the kind Rumpelstiltskin instead. Sixteen years later, their beautiful daughter, Hope, delights in traveling to town to sell golden coins spun by her father. The greedy king sees Hope and the coins and sets her to spinning gold in a cold palace cell. Using her wits, Hope persuades the king not to try to spin gold but to grow it. She convinces him to give his gold to the poor farmers, who grow food for the starving people. Her plan is so successful that she becomes the prime minister of the kingdom.

📖 *Sleepless Beauty* by Frances Minters. Illustrated by G. Brian Karas. New York: Viking, 1996.

Little Beauty is completely modern. She lives in a fancy apartment and listens to rock and roll. But she and Sleeping Beauty have one thing in common, the dreadful curse. At the age of 14, Little Beauty is doomed to prick her finger and sleep for one hundred years. But this heroine is no damsel in distress. With a little help from her favorite rock star (and setting her alarm) she is able to awaken on time and outsmart the witch.

📖 *Snow White in New York* by Fiona French. New York: Oxford University Press, 1986.

In this modern version of an old tale, Snow White is the daughter of a wealthy man. Her mother is dead. Snow White grows up surrounded by riches. Her father remarries a woman the papers dub "the classiest dame in New York." Imagine the stepmother's anger when she reads in the society column that Snow White is the "Belle of New York City." The stepmother arranges to have Snow White shot, but the girl escapes.

She wanders into a jazz club, where seven jazz men hire her as a singer. She does so well that her picture appears in the papers, where the jealous stepmother sees it. At a party for the girl the stepmother drops a poisoned cherry into a cocktail. The girl drinks it and falls to the floor, apparently dead. At the funeral one of the jazz men stumbles into the coffin and Snow White comes alive. The poisoned cherry that was stuck in her throat is gone. In the end, she marries a reporter from *The New York Times* and they sail off happily together.

Revolting Rhymes by Roald Dahl. Illustrated by Quentin Blake. New York: Alfred A. Knopf, 1982.

Here are six traditional fairy tales retold and illustrated with wicked humor. When Cinderella sees the prince chop off the heads of her stepsisters, she decides to marry a simple jam maker instead. The reason the giant smells an Englishman is because Jack never takes a bath. Using the magic mirror to tell the future, Snow White and the dwarfs clean up by betting on horses. Goldilocks turns out to be a glutton who smears the bed sheets with her messy hands. Red Riding Hood whips out her pistol, shoots the wolf, and ends up with a wolfskin coat. Since the wolf in The Three Little Pigs finds he can't blow the house down, he decides to blow it up instead. Not intended for young children, this is a clever collection of fairy tale parodies by a master storyteller.

True Story of the Three Little Pigs by Jon Scieszka. Illustrated by Lane Smith. New York: Viking, 1999.

A. Wolf describes his attempts to borrow a cup of sugar for his granny's birthday cake. He has a terrible cold and his sneezes bring down the houses of the first two pigs he visits. Comments about his granny by the third pig so anger him that he goes wild and the police are called. From his jail cell the wolf tries to explain that all he wanted was a cup of sugar.

Fairy Tales from Another Point of View by Nancy Polette. Marion, IL: Pieces of Learning, 2001.

Suppose the reason the troll wanted the goats to stay off the bridge was that the bridge was old and unsafe? How would you feel if you were a pea and the princess sat on you? Here are fairy tale plays from a point of view other than that of the protagonist.

Writing Prompt

Create a new version of a classic tale. Example:

"Henny Penny and the Acid Rain."

Reading Parts: Narrator, Henny Penny, Lazy Daisy, Chatty Patty, Silly Billy, and Gimmie Jimmy.

Narrator: A small hen was resting under a purple plum tree when the sky grew dark, the clouds tumbled over one another and warm drops of rain splashed onto her feathers. She looked. She looked again. Her feathers were turning brown. Just then Lazy Daisy walked by.

Henny Penny: Help! Help! Acid rain is coming down. My feathers are turning brown. We must tell the Mayor.

Narrator: Henny Penny and Lazy Daisy found Chatty Patty, the Mayor, putting away her garden tools.

Henny Penny and Lazy Daisy: Help! Help! Acid rain is coming down. Feathers are turning brown. Your flowers are wilting. We must tell the Vice Governor.

Narrator: Henny Penny, Lazy Daisy, and Chatty Patty found the Vice Governor, Silly Billy, mowing his lawn.

Henny Penny, Lazy Daisy, and Chatty Patty: Help! Help! Acid rain is coming down. Feathers are turning brown. Flowers are wilting. Your grass is burning up. We must tell the Governor.

Narrator: Henny Penny, Lazy Daisy, Chatty Patty, and Silly Billy set off to see the Governor, Gimmie Jimmy. His magnificent mansion sits at the edge of a green and leafy wood.

Henny Penny, Lazy Daisy, Chatty Patty, and Silly Billy: Help! Help! Acid rain is coming down. Feathers are turning brown. Flowers are wilting. Grass is burning up and your leaves are falling. We must tell the King.

Narrator: So Henny Penny, Lazy Daisy, Chatty Patty, Silly Billy, and Gimmie Jimmy set off to see the King. When the guard would not let them through the palace gates, they climbed a tall lamp post and shouted as loudly as they could:

Henny Penny, Lazy Daisy, Chatty Patty, Silly Billy, and Gimmie Jimmy: Help! Help! Acid rain is coming down. Feathers are turning brown. Flowers are wilting. Grass is burning up, leaves are falling, and the palace gates are rusting.

Narrator: But no one listened. Sure enough, the flowers wilted. The grass turned yellow and burned. The forest was filled with blackened, leafless trees, and day after day, a little brown hen sits outside the rusted palace gates crying:

Henny Penny: Help! Help! Acid rain is coming down. Help! Help! Acid rain is coming down.

Entire Cast: But no one listens.

Parody: Literary and Film

Picture Books

📖 *The Happy Hockey Family* by Lane Smith. New York: Viking, 1996.

In this parody of the Dick and Jane readers, Lane Smith puts a twist on each of 17 short tales. For example, a little girl urges her boat to float. "You can do it," she says. The boat gets the message and floats away. The little girl has to buy a new boat. Like the traditional reader, the Hockey family has a boy, a girl, a baby, and a pet. But in each adventure something goes wrong. Balloons pop, grandmother's perfume is too smelly, homework sails out the window, and a cousin breaks toys. The humor will be more appreciated by adults than children.

📖 *Kat Kong* by Dave Pilkey. San Diego: Harcourt, 1993.

In this parody of the famous movie, mice explorers led by Captain Charles Limburger reach an island where natives are offering up a sacrificial can of tuna in an attempt to placate an island monster. The small explorers manage to capture the great Kat Kong and take him by ship to Mouseopolis, making sure not to "let the cat out of the bag." There he is put on display in a theater but escapes, sending the tiny citizens of Mouseopolis into a panic. "Help," squeaks the mouse butcher, "The cat's got my tongue." Then Kat Kong spies the beautiful Rosie Rodent and takes her with him to the top of the Romano Inn. Weapons are useless against the monster until Captain Limburger flies by holding out a red package tied with gold ribbons. Reaching for the package, Kat King loses his balance and falls to his death, showing once again that "curiosity killed the cat."

📖 *Oh Brother!* by Arthur Yorinks. Illustrated by Richard Egielski. New York: Farrar, Straus & Giroux, 1989.

Oh, Brother! tells the Dickensian tale of Milton and Morris. Orphaned in New York, these intrepid young twins soon enter the school of hard knocks. Whether dangling from a circus trapeze or peddling fruit on the street, they discover that life can be harsh and bitter. But fate—in the guise of a kindly old tailor—intervenes. And, in the end, love and hope triumph over tragedy.

Writing Prompts

1. Using the style of *The Happy Hockey Family,* take a famous couple from literature (Romeo and Juliet, Heathcliff and Cathy, Jane Eyre and Rochester, etc.), write a brief scene using words that first graders could read. Example:

    My name is Romeo. I am very handsome. I like Juliet. I will climb high, high, high on a ladder to her window. I will look in the window. I see Juliet. "Hello, Juliet," I say. Juliet sees me. She says, "Go away, go away. I do not like people who look in my window. Juliet pushes the ladder. The ladder falls. I fall and break my nose. My nose is very big. I am not handsome anymore.

2. Following are motifs found in Dickens's stories:

    No one a lost child can turn to for comfort

    Starving orphans

    Death, funerals, burial grounds

    Dirty, crowded cities

    Poor children forced to work

    Street urchins who turn to crime to survive

    Work houses, orphanages

    Cruel treatment, meager food

    Lost child finds benefactor or is reunited with family

    Write a short story about a character from *A Christmas Carol*, for example, the little boy that Scrooge sees in the street on Christmas morning. Scrooge calls to the child and throws him money, asking him to go buy the Christmas goose at the butcher shop. In your story, tell who this boy is. What is he doing all alone below Scrooge's window on Christmas morning? What is his biggest problem? How will he solve it? Will Scrooge help in some way? Include as many of the listed motifs as you can.

Novels with Dickensian Themes

📖 *Black Hearts at Battersea* by Joan Aiken. New York: Doubleday, 1964.

A Dickensian mystery set in nineteenth-century London, where 15-year-old Simon uncovers a plot against King James and the Duke and Duchess of Battersea.

📖 *The Half-a-Moon Inn* by Paul Fleischman. New York: Harper, 1980.

A 12-tear-old mute boy sets off to find his mother in a blizzard and becomes a captive of an evil woman at the Half-a-Moon Inn.

📖 *The December Rose* by Leon Garfield. New York: Delacorte Press, 1988.

In Victorian London, Barnacle, a chimney sweep's assistant, finds himself pursued by the sinister Inspector Creaker.

Picture Books

📖 *The Sorcerer's Apprentice* by Ted Dewan. New York: Doubleday, 1998.

The Sorcerer is a brilliant inventor whose work keeps him so busy that he never has time to clean. If only the amazing machines he creates could pick up after themselves! Soon a clever idea is put into action, and the sorcerer invents a robot Apprentice, the perfect solution to his clutter problem. But the Apprentice, left alone in the workshop to vacuum up, has other ideas. What if he were to make his own little helper? And what if, in turn, each helper created HIS own helper? This is exactly what happens, and soon there are dozens of robots frantically rooting around for parts to make more copies, until all the tubes and wires and gears are used up. Not only that, there is no space left for the robots to move about, so they turn their nozzles on the Apprentice and on each other. Hearing the terrible fighting, the inventor leaps out of bed and runs to the workshop "He grabbed hold of the emergency power switch. He pulled down the huge handle and with a mighty BUZZ, CRACKLE, KABOOM! the robots were blown to bits." The Apprentice had learned his lesson the hard way, that sometimes machines can take control of YOU.

📖 *Swine Lake* by James Marshall. Illustrated by Maurice Sendak. New York: HarperCollins, 1999.

The "Boarshoi Ballet" is obviously a company of pigs who are performing the well-known work, "Swine Lake." The performances are held, of course, at the "New Hamsterdam" theater. This droll picture book begins with a "lean and mangy" senior citizen wolf who finds himself in front of the theater. His old nose detects the delicious aroma of pigs, "thinly disguised by French perfume." The wolf manages to get by both the ticket seller and a distracted usher and takes his seat only a short pounce from the stage. As the pig dancers begin the ballet, the hungry wolf looks closely at each one, trying to decide which would make the best meal. But as the story progresses, the wolf becomes so involved in the magic of the ballet that he decides not to pounce until the second act, then the third, and finally forgets his hunger altogether. Not only does he purchase a ticket for the next performance, but when he does leap onto the stage, the audience assumes he is a starring member of the cast and the pig dinner is completely forgotten. The power of the theater has once again worked its magic to soothe the wild beast in each of us.

📖 *Honk* by Pamela Duncan Edwards. Illustrated by Henry Cole. New York: Hyperion, 1998.

After viewing ballerinas through an opera house window, Mimi the swan falls in love with ballet. She irritates the other swans by constantly practicing. All of her attempts to enter the opera house to watch the dancers, who, incidentally, she believes are pretending to be her, are foiled until she follows a dancer through a back door and ends up on stage. Her performance is spectacular and the audience goes wild. Mimi now can enter the opera house and dance whenever she likes.

Writing Prompts

1. Using the characters from the Harry Potter books, write a short story telling how Draco Malfoy gets in trouble by trying one of Professor McGonagall's spells. He sees her cast the spell to turn her desk into a pig but does not see what she does to undo the spell. What mischief could Draco create by turning inanimate objects into some kind of animal? What would the animal(s) do? How will the spell backfire on Draco? How will Professor McGonnagall save the day?

2. Swan Lake is a well-known ballet based on an old tale about doomed lovers. A young prince falls in love with a swan maiden and vows to release her from the spell cast upon her by a wizard. The prince is tricked by the wizard into declaring his love for the wizard's daughter, thus condemning the swan maiden to a life of enchantment.

   Your story: All the birds in the fairy tale kingdom have been placed under an evil spell by a wizard. They cannot move or fly or sing. The kingdom is being overrun by bugs and beetles and all kinds of flying insects because the birds cannot catch and eat them. Choose from the following lists the characters, objects, settings, and actions you will use to release the birds from the wizard's spell.

**Who will try to
break the spell?**   **Where does the wizard live?** (choose one)

King

Queen   In a dark cave underground

Prince   In a castle guarded by ogres

Princess   In a rock fortress at the top of a mountain
                                guarded by a one-eyed giant

Youngest son   On an island in the middle of a dark lake
                                guarded by sea serpents

Poor orphan girl

(Your idea)   _____(Your idea)_____

**What magic object
can be used?**
(choose one)   **How will the spell be broken?**

Broom   By throwing water on the wizard

Invisible cloak   By learning the correct magic words to say

Magic harp   By finding a recipe for a secret brew to sprinkle
                                on the birds

Flying horse   By helping a person, bird, or other animal that
                                the sorcerer does not like

Golden bird

Magic wand

Magic brew

(Your idea)   _____(Your idea)_____

**Who will help the
main character
break the spell?**   **What will happen to the wizard at the
                                end of the story?** (choose one)
(choose one or two)

A prince or princess   He will become a good person

An old woman or man   He will change into something else

A small bird   He will disappear

A fox   He will go to another land

A fish

(Your idea)   _____(Your idea)_____

About Swan Lake

Tchaikovsky's famous ballet tells the story of the Swan Queen Odette and her lover, Prince Siegfried, who is tricked by the evil magician Rothbart into breaking his vow of fidelity. One ballerina usually dances the dual roles of Odette and the impostor Odile. The role requires both dramatic skills and outstanding technique and is one of the most coveted and demanding roles in the classical repertory. It is considered a yardstick by which a ballerina must prove herself.

Parody: Mother Goose

Picture Books

📖 *The Inner City Mother Goose* by Eve Merriam. New York: Simon & Schuster, reissue 1996.

This highly controversial collection of verse often appears on banned lists. The author, in her introduction, states that her purpose in presenting these thought-provoking rhymes is to raise public awareness of the problems of the inner city. "Now I lay me down to sleep" requires double locks to keep robbers out. Mary grows a sidewalk instead of a garden. The sidewalk grows tons of refuse because of a garbage strike. Diddle Diddle Dumpling shares a bed with his family in a one-room flat. Little Jack Horner fails to learn to read because the reader he is given contains nothing to which he can relate. The problems are as real as the verse is biting. Both should make the reader uncomfortable.

📖 *The Thinker's Mother Goose* by Nancy Polette. Illustrated by Jerry Warshaw. O'Fallon, MO: Book Lures, 1990.

Many members of Mother Goose's family have problems. Some try to solve them: Miss Muffet runs away when bothered by a spider. Some can't solve them: Humpty Dumpty couldn't be put together again. This collection of rhymes offers solutions to the problems faced by Mother Goose characters. A lady magician puts Humpty Dumpty together again; Miss Muffet solves her problem by dumping her curds and whey on the spider. Jill vows never again to climb a hill with her abusive brother, and Jack Be Nimble learns to fly. As for Mother Goose, when she wants to wander, she trades in her goose for a jumbo jet plane. A second verse added to the original shows how fun creative problem solving can be.

Whatever Happened to Humpty Dumpty?: And Other Surprising Sequels to Mother Goose Rhymes by David Greenberg. Illustrated by S. D. Schindler. Boston: Little, Brown, 1999.

Not intended for very young children, this collection of rhymes speculates on the fate of many Mother Goose characters. Humpty Dumpty nearly experiences being a giant omelet but instead ends up on the kitchen wall. Jack Be Nimble is burned to ash. Jack and Jill are flushed down the toilet. Mother Goose and her gander end up in heaven after a collision with a 747. When Peter's wife emerges from her pumpkin shell, she sticks Peter in a loaf of bread. Cartoon-style artwork accompanies the rhymes.

Writing Prompts

Read a variety of Mother Goose rhymes. Study Eve Merriam's rhymes to point out a current problem in society. Examples:

OLD MOTHER GOOSE
Old mother goose
When she wanted to wander
Would fly through the air
On a very fine gander.
When she crashes
The world will come back
Until her next high
With her passenger, Crack.

PETER, PETER, PUMPKIN EATER
Peter, Peter, pumpkin eater,
Had a wife and couldn't keep her.
Welfare check was not enough
To give her food and clothes and stuff.

For another version, determine the problem of a Mother Goose character. Decide on a solution. Reveal your solution in a second verse. Example:

> LADY BIRD, LADY BIRD
> Lady bird, Lady bird
> Fly away home
> Your house is on fire
> Your children are gone
> Look by the stove
> And see little Ann
> She has crept under
> The warming pan.
> A bad place to be
> With the house
> Up in flames
> The telephone book has no
> "Fire Put Out" names
> And Ann, she is yelling
> She's really gone wild
> So call 911
> To rescue the child.

"Paul Revere" Poetry

Picture Books

Iron Horses by Verla Kay. Illustrated by Michael McCurdy. New York: Putnam, 2000.

In what is sometimes termed " Paul Revere" poetry (because it moves so quickly), Verla Kay tells the story of the building of the transcontinental railroad from its conception to the meeting of the rails from east to west in Utah. The rapidly moving text gives the feeling of the train moving along faster and faster, "Thumping, bumping, ties and rails, Clanging, banging, Spikes and nails." The excitement builds as the back-breaking work accelerates, through blazing heat and bitter cold, with Irish and Chinese working together to make a dream a reality.

📖 *Covered Wagons, Bumpy Trails* by Verla Kay. Illustrated by S. D. Schindler. New York: Putnam, 2000.

"Covered wagon, Bumpy road, Plodding oxen, Heavy load." A pioneer family heads west. They stuff all of their belongings into their wagon and start on their way to build a new life in California's Sacramento Valley. Deep rivers, endless pains, steep mountains, and even a desert are in their way, but this pioneer family is determined to make it. Wagon trains needed to reach Independence Rock by the Fourth of July to get through the mountains before winter hits, and the average speed of a fully loaded wagon was 15 miles per day. A map showing the route from Independence, Missouri, to the Sacramento Valley is included. The spirit of the grueling and exciting life on those treacherous trails comes alive through the buoyant verse of Verla Kay. The author's notes show the careful research that supports every detail in both text and illustrations.

Writing Prompt

Choose an incident from history. Research the details and write about it using the "Paul Revere" poetry similar to that used in these two books. See a true account of how Tad Lincoln saved the Thanksgiving turkey from a White House feast in the following example:

> *How Tad Lincoln Saved the White House Turkey*
> For Thanksgiving
> Holiday
> Big fat turkey
> Came to stay
> White House
> Dinner
> Table Set
> Cooking up
> Tad's
> Turkey pet
> Tad refused
> Its life
> To end
> For the
> Turkey was

His friend.
Into chambers
Young Tad went
Interrupted
The President.
Please, Sir
I don't want
Him killed.
President
Nodded
Voice was stilled.
Stop the
Pleading
Do not
Grieve
Here's a
President's
Reprieve.
Turkey's life
Was to be
Spared.
Lincoln showed
He really
Cared.

Puns

Picture Books

📖 *Ding Dong, Ding Dong* by Margie Palatini. New York: Hyperion, 1999.

Surviving as a door-to-door salesman for Ape-on Cosmetics turns out to be quite a challenge for one determined chimp, even though he has a degree in Monkey Business. Luckily, the Big Guy has more than a little savvy, and with "no more monkeying around," he heads straight for the Big City. It is not long before this oversized galoot makes for the tallest building around and, setting his sights high, "works his way up" in the world with a pail and squeegee. Looking through a window in the 81st floor, the chimp goes into his sales pitch and gets a smile from a lady. He figures now he has her in "the palm of his hand" but gets dizzy, takes a tumble, and finds himself looking at a Hollywood talent agent who signs him up to be a box office KING. Older students will enjoy the plays on words and recognize the many cultural and commercial references.

📖 *Hoots and Toots and Hairy Brutes* by Larry Shles. Rolling Hills Estates, CA: Jalmar, 1984.

The master of the visual and verbal pun does it again with this tale of Squib, a small owl who cannot hoot. The only thing that comes out when he opens his beak is a tiny toot. His concerned parents take him to the orthodontist, who says he is suffering from "overbeak" and recommends a retainer which, when removed, does not solve the problem. The parents then hire a tutor, which puzzles Squib. He knows how to toot; he thinks they should have hired a "hooter." Nothing that is tried is successful, but Squib's tiny toot saves the day when a hunter, the "hairy brute," threatens his parents. Many readers are inspired to play with owl puns. Examples: What monument do owls visit? The Statue of Squiberty. What owls dance at Radio City? The Squibettes. How would you describe an owl who has just had a bath? Clean owl over.

📖 *Nose Drops* by Larry Shles. St. Louis, MO: Squib Publications, 1994.

Geoffrey is a nose that has no face. He wonders what will become of him. Without a face he is sure he will never become a famous scientist like " Dr. Hypotanose" or a great leader like Julius Sneezer. He will never make the covers of "Snorts Illustrated" or "Noseweek." But Geoffrey does become one of the most famous noses in all of history in this pun-filled story of his life.

Writing Prompt

Puns are plays on words that are created by changing just a few letters. Try writing "punny" riddles.

1. Select a subject. Example: hippopotamus.

2. List words that end with the letters IP. Example: *slip, drip, clip.*

3. Ask a question. Examples:

    -   What would you call a hippopotamus that steps on a banana peel? A slippopotamus.

    -   What would you call a hippopotamus with a runny nose? A drippopotamus.

    -   A hippopotamus barber is a clippopotamus.

Try punny riddles for caterpillar (words that end in "at"), rattlesnake (words that end in "at"), or cockroach (words that end in "ock").

The Quest Tale

Picture Book

📖 *Pondlarker* by Fred Gwynne. New York: Simon & Schuster, 1990.

The hero of this tale is a small frog who longs for bigger things in his world and sets out on a journey to find them. Meeting difficulties along the way, he finally reaches his goal, only to find a surprise.

Writing Prompt

Follow the directions below in outlining a quest tale. Compare your outline with the actions and events in *Pondlarker*.

1. Stage One: The Call to Action

   - You are a young male frog and you feel you are different from all the other frogs in your pond.

   - Give reasons why you feel you are different.

   - You also feel that you must go on a quest. What will you seek?

   - Your parents try to convince you not to go. Tell what your parents say.

2. Stage Two: The Initiation

   - You go anyway. On your quest you encounter two difficult situations. Tell what they are and also how you overcome them.

   - You find the object of your quest. Describe it.

   - When you approach the object of your quest, you are startled and amazed at what you see. Tell what you see.

   - You decide not to take that which you had sought. Explain why.

3.   Stage Three: The Return

- You return to the pond. Explain why.

- Your parents and friends greet you. Describe what they say.

- You have learned an important lesson. State what it is.

Repetition

Picture Book

📖 *The Iron Giant* by Ted Hughes. Illustrated by Dirk Zimmer. New York: HarperCollins, 1968.

The Iron Giant came to the top of the cliff. How far had he come? Nobody knows. Where had he come from? Nobody knows. Ted Hughes, former Poet Laureate of Great Britain, uses the tools of the poet in this narrative tale of a giant who is tricked by townspeople and led into a deep pit. When, however, a creature from outer space threatens the Earth and all of the weapons the people have built are to no avail, the Iron Giant manages to save the Earth from destruction. The text abounds with metaphor, personification, and repetition.

Writing Prompt

Note how Ted Hughes uses repetition in describing action. Choose an action to describe and use repetition to make your description more powerful. Example:

> His right foot, his enormous right foot lifted . . . his iron legs fell off. His iron arms broke off, and the hands broke off the arms. His great iron ears fell off, and his eyes fell out. His great iron head fell off.

Choose:

- The wind in your face on a motorcycle ride.
- Sitting on the top of a ferris wheel.
- A walk to the principal's office.
- Surfing a wave.
- A race horse near the finish line.

Similes

Picture Book

📖 *A Surfeit of Similes* by Norton Juster. New York: Morrow Junior Books, 1989.

What's as still as a statue, as busy as bees, as scary as heights, as silly as knees? What else but a simile, a figure of speech as clever as zippers, as fresh as a peach. So, if you're tired of books that are as much fun as a sharp pebble in your shoe or as exciting as a plateful of cabbage, then try this one. It's as keen as a razor in verse and in rhyme, as bright as a penny, you'll have a good time.

Writing Prompt

Choose a topic and compose similes related to the topic. Combine your similes in verse form. Example:

A dove is like a warm winged snowball.

A snake is like a wiggling piece of water laughing silently across the ground.

Empty picture frames are like tents with no people.

A toothache is like sleet scratching across a winter window.

Bottles breaking are like my sister yelling in the basement.

My purring cat is like a motorcycle at a stoplight.

Our ringing phone is like steel marbles talking together in the wall.

Allow the mind

to range far and wide
 like a cowboy riding a star,

to plumb great depths
 like a dolphin diving into a rose,

to soar beyond the known universe
 like an astronaut dancing into space on the strings of a violin,

to fall onto the page
 *like raindrops bursting
 into the singing shapes of letter-perfect swans.*

Keith Polette

Story Starters

Picture Book

📖 *Mysteries of Harris Burdick* by Chris Van Allsburg. Boston: Houghton Mifflin, 1984.

When Chris Van Allsburg is invited to the home of Peter Wenders, he discovers 14 drawings that are, like pieces of a picture puzzle, clues to larger pictures. But the puzzles, the mysteries, presented by these drawings are not what we are used to. They are not solved for us, as in the final pages of a book or a film's last reel. The solutions to these mysteries lie in a place at once closer at hand yet far more remote. They lie in the imagination.

A middle-aged man holds a chair over his head, staring at a large lump under the living room rug. The picture is titled "Under the Rug." The caption reads, "Two weeks passed and it happened again." A picture of a nun floating in a chair high up in a cathedral is titled "The Seven

Chairs" and captioned, "The fifth one ended up in France." For those who have thought of themselves as unimaginative, this book will prove the opposite. Even the most reluctant imagination, when confronted by these drawings, will not be able to resist solving the mysteries of Harris Burdick.

Writing Prompt

Use the illustrations and first lines in the book to stimulate the imagination. Write what happens next. Example:

Under the Rug

Judge Jones stared in disbelief. The lump under the courtroom rug grew larger and larger. It swelled like a huge boil ready to burst. Then another lump appeared beside the first and still another and another. Each lump wiggled round and round like a belly dancer. Then slowly the rug pulled from the wall. Inch by inch it crept toward the wiggling lumps. In a sudden flash of movement the rug was thrown aside to reveal four moving bodies with arms reaching to pull themselves from four dark holes. The prisoners the Judge had sentenced to life had dug a tunnel from the jail not realizing that their miscalculations would bring once again face to face with the Judge!

Tone Poem

Picture Book

📖 *Listen to the Rain* by Bill Martin Jr. and John Archambault. Illustrated by James Endicott. New York: Henry Holt, 1989.

In this illustrated tone poem, Bill Martin Jr. and John Archambault evoke the beauty and the mystery, the sounds and the silences, of rain. The rain begins with a whisper and the first sprinkles are barely heard. In the second stanza the rain increases to a SONG! It sings with a steady beat and lulls one into a feeling of contentment. In the third stanza the storm hits with all its fury and the "roaring, pouring" rain falls amid the flashes of lightning and roar of thunder. In the final stanza the rain has stopped and we now hear the soft dripping of drops from the trees. Study the beautiful style of this book. Notice the sounds and movements that are created with words.

Writing Prompt

Use this pattern to create your own "Listen to the Wind" poem. Example:

> Listen to the wind
> The murmur of the wind
> A slow torch song
> As it moves along
> The quiet murmur of the wind.

AUTHOR/ILLUSTRATOR AND TITLE INDEX

117

ABOUT THE AUTHORS

Nancy Polette is Professor Emeritus of Education at Lindenwood University and the author of over 100 professional books, including *Exploring Books with Gifted Children*, *Three Rs for the Gifted*, and *Gifted Books, Gifted Readers*. She is an in-demand speaker at national and state library, gifted, and reading conferences and serves as a consultant in reading, writing, and research for school districts throughout the United States and Canada.

Joan Ebbesmeyer has over 30 years' experience in education serving as a classroom teacher, director of gifted programs, and adjunct professor at the University of Missouri, Rolla, and Lindenwood University. She is the author of *Exploring the Classics* and *The Middle Ages*. Joan divides her time among teaching, writing, and conducting workshops for educators in critical and creative thinking.

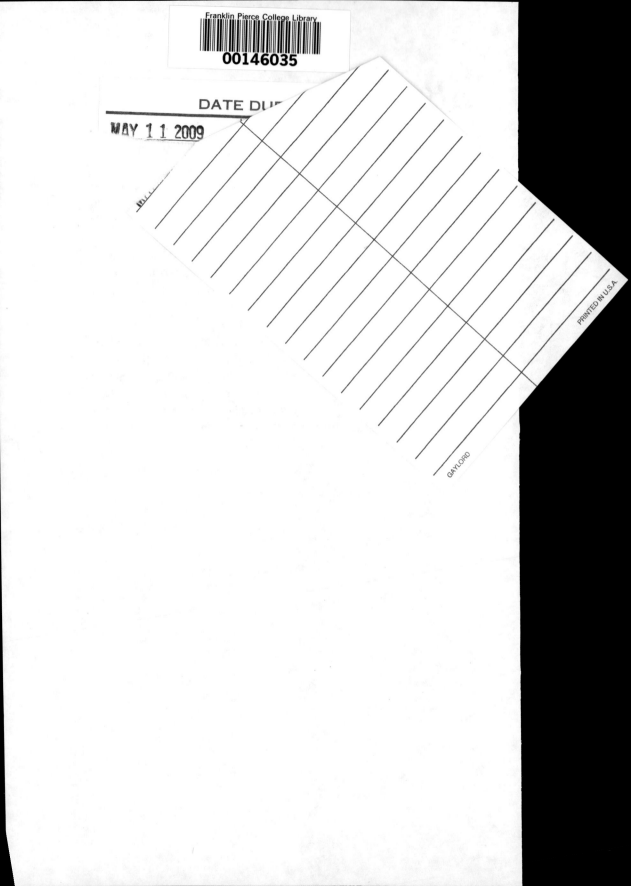